THE
OVERCOMERS

A Bible Study in the Book of Revelation

BIBLE STUDY GUIDE | EIGHT SESSIONS

MATT CHANDLER

WITH DUDLEY J. DELFFS

HarperChristian Resources

The Overcomers Bible Study Guide
© 2024 Matt Chandler

Published in Grand Rapids, Michigan, by HarperChristian Resources. HarperChristian Resources is a registered trademark of HarperCollins Christian Publishing, Inc.

Requests for information should be sent to customercare@harpercollins.com.

ISBN: 978-0-310-16534-7 (softcover)
ISBN: 978-0-310-16535-4 (e-book)

All Scripture quotations, unless otherwise indicated, are taken from The Holy Bible, New International Version®, NIV®. Copyright © 1973, 1978, 1984, 2011 by Biblica, Inc.® Used by permission of Zondervan. All rights reserved worldwide. www.Zondervan.com. The "NIV" and "New International Version" are trademarks registered in the United States Patent and Trademark Office by Biblica, Inc.®

Scripture quotations marked ESV are taken from the ESV® Bible (The Holy Bible, English Standard Version®). Copyright © 2001 by Crossway, a publishing ministry of Good News Publishers. Used by permission. All rights reserved.

Scripture quotations marked TLB are taken from The Living Bible copyright © 1971 by Tyndale House Foundation. Used by permission of Tyndale House Publishers Inc., Carol Stream, Illinois 60188. All rights reserved.

Italics in Scripture quotations are the emphasis of the author.

Any internet addresses (websites, blogs, etc.) and telephone numbers in this study guide are offered as a resource. They are not intended in any way to be or imply an endorsement by HarperChristian Resources, nor does Harper-Christian Resources vouch for the content of these sites and numbers for the life of this study guide.

All rights reserved. No portion of this book may be reproduced, stored in a retrieval system, or transmitted in any form or by any means—electronic, mechanical, photocopy, recording, scanning, or other—except for brief quotations in critical reviews or articles, without the prior written permission of the publisher.

HarperChristian Resources titles may be purchased in bulk for church, business, fundraising, or ministry use. For information, please e-mail ResourceSpecialist@ChurchSource.com.

Published in association with Yates & Yates (www.yates2.com).

First printing March 2024 / Printed in the United States of America

CONTENTS

A NOTE FROM MATT

It's easy to become overwhelmed in today's world. So much comes at you on any given day. Technology, online connectivity, and social media allow you to access world events as they happen in ways that were impossible for previous generations. You are constantly flooded with the latest headlines from global leaders, popular entertainers, and celebrity influencers—along with news of the latest pandemics, natural disasters, and economic turbulence.

If you are a follower of Jesus, you know that God wants you to rely on His Word for stability during these tumultuous times. You recognize that the Bible provides instruction, insight, and inspiration for how you are to live *in* this world while not being a part *of* it (see John 17:14-15). But some parts of God's Word just seem clearer than others—and perhaps no other book in Scripture causes more misunderstanding than the book of Revelation. In fact, it wouldn't be a stretch to say that this uniquely strange, beautiful, and awesome book might just be the *most* frequently misquoted and misunderstood book in the Bible.

The enemy has certainly had a hand in this. If he can convince you that Revelation is too mysterious to be understood, then he can rob you of the hope that empowers your faith and emboldens your courage in adversity. If he can get you to avoid Revelation, then he can steal your understanding of how to live triumphantly over his schemes and plans. If he can get you caught up in asking questions like whether the latest vaccine is the mark of the beast, or a particular politician is the Antichrist, or global pandemics like Covid-19 represent the pale horse mentioned in Revelation 6, then he can distract you from the most important truth of the book—that God is sovereign over human history and your victory has already been won.

In truth, the *central* message of Revelation is all about the dynamic and empowered life that God intends you to have—and the life you want for yourself. In spite of what you see happening around you, God is at work accomplishing His purposes in the mess and madness of your everyday life. He is seeking and saving the lost, exacting justice on His creation, working miracles among the sick and brokenhearted, and pouring out His mercy and grace.

God knows how overwhelming and scary this world can be. So He gave you a picture of your ultimate reality in the book of Revelation. This picture has strengthened and encouraged countless Christians across the ages. It can do the same for you.

As a companion to *The Overcomers* book, this study will help you understand this picture, know your place in God's divine purposes, and recognize why Satan is terrified that you have this in your hands right now. You are uniquely wired and precisely placed in this moment in human history as part of God's plan to push back the darkness and establish the light.

If you want to live as an overcomer, the book Revelation is your key. So, are you ready to dive in and explore everthing this book has to offer? Then let's get started!

– MATT CHANDLER

HOW TO USE THIS GUIDE

The book of Revelation remains timeless in its power and relevancy. For more than two centuries, it has encouraged and empowered followers of Jesus, helping them push back the darkness of the enemy and establish order and light. Your spiritual predecessors faced all kinds of adversity and persecution, yet the truth and hope found in Revelation sustained them.

In this study, you will see the same is available for you. Through the Spirit-inspired message, language, and images found in Revelation, God wants you to understand the fullness of who you are and what your divine purpose is. He wants you to know and live out the truth of being made in His image, of being His beloved child, and of being uniquely wired and intentionally placed where you are right now. God wants you to step into your design and destiny and embrace all that you are intended to be.

So, with this in mind, know that there are a few ways that you can go through this material. You can experience this study with others in a small group (such as a Bible study, Sunday school class, or home group), or you may choose to go through the content on your own. Either way, the videos for each session are available for you to view at any time by following the instructions provided with this study guide.

GROUP STUDY

Each session is divided into two parts: (1) a group study section, and (2) a personal study section. The group study section provides a basic framework on how to open your time together, get the most out of the video content, and discuss the key ideas together that were presented in the teaching. Each session includes the following:

- **Welcome:** A short note about the topic of the session for you to read on your own before you meet as a group.

- **Connect:** A few icebreaker questions to get you and your group members thinking about the topic and interacting with each other.
- **Watch:** An outline of the key points covered in each video teaching to help you follow along, stay engaged, and take notes.
- **Discuss:** Questions to help your group reflect on the teaching material presented and apply it to your lives.
- **Respond:** A short personal exercise to help you reinforce the key ideas.
- **Pray:** A place for you to record prayer requests and praises for the week.

If you are doing this study in a group, make sure you have your own copy of this study guide so you can write down your thoughts, responses, and reflections and have access to the videos via streaming. You will also want to have a copy of *The Overcomers*, as reading it alongside the curriculum will provide you with deeper insights. (See the notes at the beginning of each group session and personal study section on which chapters of the book you should read before the next group session.) Finally, keep these points in mind:

- **Facilitation:** If you are doing this study in a group, you will want to appoint someone to serve as a facilitator. This person will be responsible for starting the video and keeping track of time during discussions and activities. If *you* have been chosen for this role, there are some resources in the back of this guide that can help you lead your group through the study.

- **Faithfulness:** Your group is a place where tremendous growth can happen as you reflect on the Bible, ask questions, and learn what God is doing in other people's lives. For this reason, be fully committed and attend each session so you can build trust and rapport with the other members.

- **Friendship:** The goal of any small group is to serve as a place where people can share, learn about God, and build friendships. So seek to make your group a "safe place." Be honest about your thoughts and feelings, but also listen carefully to everyone else's thoughts, feelings, and opinions. Keep anything personal that your group members share in confidence so that you can create a community where people can heal, be challenged, and grow spiritually.

If you are going through this study on your own, read the opening Welcome section and reflect on the questions in the Connect section. Watch the video and use the prompts provided to take notes. Finally, personalize the questions and exercises in the Discuss and Respond sections. Close by recording any requests you want to pray about during the week.

PERSONAL STUDY

The personal study is for you to work through on your own during the week. Each exercise is designed to help you explore the key ideas you uncovered during your group time and delve into passages of Scripture that will help you apply those principles to your life. Go at your own pace, doing a little each day—or tackle the material all at once. Remember to spend a few moments in silence to listen to whatever the Holy Spirit might be saying to you.

Each section contains three personal studies that open with a brief devotion for you to read, a few passages for you to look up, and several reflection questions to help you apply the truths of God's Word to your life. Following this, there is a Connect & Discuss page with several questions for you to answer with a friend, either over a phone call or a cup of coffee. Finally, the Catch Up & Read Ahead page will give you a chance to finish any uncompleted personal studies and read the upcoming chapters in Revelation and *The Overcomers*.

If you are doing this study as part of a group and are unable to finish (or even start) these personal studies for the week, you should still attend the group time. Be assured that you are wanted and welcome even if you don't have your "homework" done. The group and personal studies are intended to help you hear what God wants you to hear and learn how to apply it to your life. So as you go through this study, be listening for what God has to say to you as an overcomer. Whether you face good times or hard times, when you focus on Jesus, you will experience renewed hope and power to overcome every challenge and struggle.

WEEK 1

BEFORE GROUP MEETING	Read Revelation 1–3 Review chapters 1–2 in *The Overcomers* Read the Welcome section (page 2)
GROUP MEETING	Discuss the Connect questions Watch the video teaching for session 1 Discuss the questions that follow as a group Do the closing exercise and pray (pages 2–6)
STUDY 1	Complete the personal study (pages 9–11)
STUDY 2	Complete the personal study (pages 12–14)
STUDY 3	Complete the personal study (pages 15–17)
CONNECT & DISCUSS	Connect with someone in your group (page 18)
CATCH UP AND READ AHEAD (BEFORE WEEK 2 GROUP MEETING)	Read Revelation 4–5 Review chapters 3–4 in *The Overcomers* Complete any unfinished personal studies (page 19)

YOU WERE MADE FOR THIS DAY

Blessed is the one who reads aloud the words of this prophecy, and blessed are those who hear it and take to heart what is written in it, because the time is near.

REVELATION 1:3

WELCOME | READ ON YOUR OWN

Imagine finding a letter that one of your ancestors wrote decades ago. Although it was addressed to family members back then, you find that it speaks to your life today. Strangely enough, it reminds you of who you are—the origins of your family, the struggles that have been overcome, and the timeless shared values that you all still hold. You feel part of a bigger family picture after reading it and gain a better idea of where you fit in your family tree.

Reading Revelation has a similar impact on believers. Yes, it is an intimidating book with, frankly, a lot of weird characters in it. Yet for more than 2,000 years, it has instilled courage in the lives of Christians throughout the world, regardless of the time period in which they lived. God's message in Revelation spoke to believers when it was first written, assuring them that in spite of what they were experiencing in the world, Jesus was on His throne and ruling on high. They could live boldly and confidently, knowing that God had set them in a divinely appointed time and place.

Reading Revelation will provide the same reassurance for you. You can know without a doubt that *you* were made for this day. In this opening session, you will get an overview of what Revelation is and what it is not. As you will see, John, the author of the book, tells you up front what Revelation is all about. Right out of the gate, you will see that Revelation was a letter written to a specific group of people living at a specific time and in a specific place—similar to Paul's letters that you find in Ephesians, Philippians, and Romans. Keeping this in mind provides perspective: Revelation was written *for* you as a believer, but it was not written *to* you.

CONNECT | 15 MINUTES

If any of your group members don't know each other, take a few minutes to introduce yourselves. Then discuss one or both of the following questions:

- Why did you decide to join this study? What do you hope to learn?

  — *or* —

- What is your general view on the world you live in today? What words best describe your sense of the time and place in which you are living?

WATCH | 20 MINUTES

Read Revelation 1–3 before you watch the video teaching, which you can access by playing the DVD or through streaming (see the instructions provided with this study guide).

OUTLINE

I. John wrote Revelation c. AD 96 to seven churches in the province of Asia (see 1:4).
   A. Revelation is written *for* us but not *to* us.
   B. John references the Old Testament at least 500 times—the original recipients would have recognized these references.
   C. Revelation does not say something to us that it did not say to its original recipients.

II. Contextually, the seven churches faced immense cultural pressure and political persecution.
   A. Christians were imprisoned, tortured, and killed under Emperor Nero in AD 65. This continued under Emperor Vespasian in AD 67.
   B. Church morale suffered with the destruction of Jerusalem in AD 70 and the deaths of Peter, Paul, and Timothy.
   C. In AD 92, Emperor Domitian ordered all Roman citizens to worship him and legally required Christians to renounce their faith.

III. John categorized the seven churches into three distinct types.
   A. Biblically knowledgeable but cold (Ephesus).
   B. Spiritually aware but indifferent (Pergamum, Thyatira, Sardis, and Laodicea).
   C. Spiritually weary and falling away (Smyrna and Philadelphia).

IV. Revelation is biblical prophecy (see 1:3). It focuses more on "thus says the Lord" and less on "this is what is coming."
   A. We must resist the inclination to read Revelation as a linear or chronological story.
   B. Revelation presents a series of visions that progress in the order that John saw them.
   C. Consequently, the question is not "What happened next?" but rather "What did John see next?"

V. Revelation is apocalyptic literature (see 1:1). It uses symbolic imagery to inform our minds and ignite our hearts.
   A. The word we translate as Revelation is *apocalypsis*, which means "unveiling" or "disclosure."
   B. Revelation "unveiled" to the seven churches in Asia—and to us—that there is more in the spiritual realms than believers can see.
   C. Similar to other Old Testament books, Revelation conveys its message with imagery and symbolism, including colors and numbers.

NOTES

DISCUSS | 35 MINUTES

Discuss what you just watched by answering the following questions.

1. What three kinds of literary genres does the book of Revelation reflect? Why is it important to understand each type in order to grasp the meaning of Revelation?

2. John categorized the seven churches into three types: (1) biblically knowledgeable but cold, (2) spiritually aware but indifferent, and (3) spiritually weary and falling away. How do you think the cultural and political persecutions of the day titled each of the churches toward one or more of these categories that John describes?

3. Which of the three kinds of churches that you read about in Revelation 2–3 seems worse than the others? Why?

4. Revelation is a *biblical prophecy*. How would you define and describe the prophetic books or prophetic parts of the Bible? In terms of purpose and impact, what is the difference between "thus says the Lord" and "this is what is coming"?

5. How does understanding the characteristics of apocalyptic literature change your overall impression of the book of Revelation? Why does it change your perception of the book in that way?

RESPOND | 10 MINUTES

As you consider how Revelation applies to you, it will help to keep the big picture in mind. John begins with this foundational perspective by immediately identifying who he is, what he is writing, why he is writing, and how he received this message: "The revelation from Jesus Christ, which God gave him to show his servants what must soon take place. He made it known by sending his angel to his servant John, who testifies to everything he saw—that is, the word of God and the testimony of Jesus Christ" (Revelation 1:1–2). He then states the desired impact of his message: "Blessed is the one who reads aloud the words of this prophecy, and blessed are those who hear it and take to heart what is written in it, because the time is near" (verse 3).

How does John's opening help you understand the overall purpose of Revelation?

Why do you think John chose to state the impact that he hoped his message would have? How does this impact go beyond the seven churches to include you?

What does it mean for you to "take to heart" the "words of this prophecy" right now?

PRAY | 10 MINUTES

Praying for one another is one of the most important things you can do as a community. So use this prayer time as a way to support, encourage, and uplift one another rather than just as a "closing prayer" to end your group experience. Be intentional about sharing your prayer requests, reviewing how God is answering your prayers and praying for each other as a group. As you pray, ask God to use the message of Revelation to reassure you and to strengthen your faith. Before you close your session, write down any requests so that you and your fellow group members can continue to pray about them in the week ahead.

PERSONAL STUDY

As you heard during the group time, the book of Revelation still speaks to you today. In particular, it can help clarify your spiritual perspective and renew your passion for Jesus when cultural trends and worldly pressures tempt you to compromise. This week, you will look at a few verses that will help you engage with this extraordinary book and consider how your struggles parallel some of the same challenges faced by believers in the seven churches. As you consider these passages, ask God to reveal what He wants you to learn. He has something specific for you to take away from this study! Be sure to write down your responses as you work through these questions, as you will be given a few minutes to share your insights if you are doing this study with a group. If you are reading *The Overcomers* alongside this study, you may find it helpful to complete or review chapters 1–2 in the book.

OPEN THE LETTER

You live in a time when most people communicate by text, DM (direct message), and social media, so you may find the notion of a handwritten letter somewhat quaint, old-fashioned, and obsolete. Nevertheless, ever since the advent of written language, people have corresponded by putting pen or pencil to some form of paper. In the words of Ida Tomshimsky, a twenty-first century communications historian, "According to the testimony of ancient historian Hellanicus, the first recorded handwritten letter . . . was written by Persian Queen Atossa, around 500 BC."[1]

Most experts agree that early letter writing was generally motivated by three purposes: (1) to conduct business, (2) to correspond personally, and (3) to publicly announce royal or governmental decrees and rules. Animals, including pigeons and horses, were often used to deliver early letters, as were human messengers, particularly traveling merchants, tradesmen, and soldiers. Eventually, the use of a regional postal system developed during the early sixteenth century in what is now the United Kingdom, with letters being addressed to individuals and then relayed to a central location for distribution and delivery.[2]

To the best of our knowledge, the letter we know today as Revelation did not arrive by carrier pigeon or mail carrier. Just like the other letters in the Bible (also called epistles), Revelation was written by one person and intended for a specific audience. The recipients—a church in this case—would likely have heard the letter read to them as a group. While we don't know with certainty how the letter of Revelation was delivered to the specific congregations addressed, it is clear that John was writing to the seven churches of Asia (see 1:4).

Before John identified himself and his audience, he established the source of the message he would reveal. This was not just any letter to any recipient. *Jesus* had sent an angel to John to convey the message the he had for these churches. In response, John was testifying to everything he saw—"the word of God and the testimony of Jesus Christ" (verse 2).

READ | Revelation 1:1–5; Jeremiah 1:1–10; Romans 1:1–7

REFLECT

1. When was the last time you wrote a personal letter to someone? For what purpose did you write it? What was John's purpose in writing his letter (see Revelation 1:1)?

2. What compelled John to write his letter (see verses 1–2)? What compelled the prophet Jeremiah to write the words of his book (see Jeremiah 1:1–10)?

> John was well known to the churches of Asia and used similar language in his Gospel and other letters as he does in Revelation: Jesus is the Word of God, the Lamb of God, and Living Water. This is important to understand because this book was written for a specific group of people in a particular place at a particular time. This truth should help you understand what God wants to say to you. He cannot say something to you here that He wasn't saying to them. Revelation was written *to* them but *for* you.[3]

3. John described himself simply as a "servant" of Jesus (see Revelation 1:1). How did Paul describe himself in his letter to the church in Rome (see Romans 1:1–7)?

> When our Christian family in the first century said, "Jesus is Lord," they made a countercultural statement. They were standing in stark opposition at that moment. And now it's our turn. The message of the book of Revelation is meant to bring stability in the most challenging times imaginable. It also brings

strength and comfort to those subject to the usual temptations and minor sacrifices that following Jesus will bring. When you feel the pull to withdraw, to check out, or to doubt your relevance at this moment, the Lord wants to flood your soul with courage and joy from on high through the book of Revelation.[4]

4. Does it surprise you to learn that Revelation is meant to provide stability and reassurance in the midst of the challenges you may be facing? Why or why not?

5. Write a letter to God concerning both your expectations and concerns for studying the book of Revelation. Be honest about any fears or apprehensions you may have. Conclude by asking for the Holy Spirit to guide you throughout this study.

Dear God . . .

PRAY | End your time in prayer. Thank God for the opportunity to study His Word and ask Him to open the eyes of your heart. Be sure to listen for anything He may want you to know.

DIVINE DECLARATION

Weather forecasters typically report current conditions before predicting weather patterns that seem likely in days to come. They describe present variables with certainty, while tomorrow's forecast relies on what they *expect* to happen. In some ways, prophecy is not so different.

Revelation, in addition to being John's letter to seven churches, is also biblical prophecy. Now, when you see the word *prophecy*, you might assume it is the same as "future-telling," or describing what will happen at some point beyond the present. While there are certainly examples in the Bible of God giving insights about future events to certain people, the prophets generally conveyed God's divine declarations.

In other words, rather than future-telling, God's prophets (particularly in the Old Testament) typically called His people to obedience and warned of what would happen if they did not heed the message. Biblical prophecy might thus be considered *divine declaration* rather than *prescribed prediction*. God called on His chosen messengers to relay what He wanted His chosen people, the Israelites, to know.

We see these kinds of declarations made by prophets such as Isaiah, Jeremiah, and Ezekiel. Their books contain future-telling passages, but their main message boils down to "thus says the Lord." These prophets condemned the depravity of their day while calling the people to repentance. Their prophetic messages were intended to compel the people of God to walk in holiness, reject the evil and rebellion of their day, and rely on God rather than their own abilities or the ways of the world.

The book of Revelation is thus a "prophecy" in the sense that it is God's declaration to His people—a panoramic view of His eternal and ultimate reality rather than solely a description of future events. In truth, one of the primary purposes of Revelation, as a prophetic declaration, is to call believers—both the original recipients and us today—to holiness. Rather than compromising to a predominant culture known for rejecting and even mocking Jesus' reign and rule, Christians are set apart, sanctified, and empowered for God's purposes.

READ | Revelation 2:1–3:22; Jeremiah 19:1–6; Ezekiel 6:1–6

REFLECT

1. In the Old Testament, God sometimes related future events through His prophets, but more often His purpose was to relate His divine declarations through them. How do you see God using Jeremiah and Ezekiel in this manner (see Jeremiah 19:1–6; Ezekiel 6:1–6)?

2. What common elements are in John's prophecy to the churches? How would you describe the message that Jesus is giving to them (see Revelation 2:1–3:22)?

In most cases, the people of God are shaken by the moral and social decline occurring in their day. You and I are witnessing this before our eyes as our present reality is hyper-sexualized, violent, and increasingly hostile to the picture of moral beauty we see in the Scriptures. Many Christians are afraid to say anything that might make them the target of an internet mob or create friction at work or in the neighborhood. (I'm not saying this is your role as much as I am highlighting what a prophet did.)[5]

3. Do you believe that the purpose of biblical prophecy remains the same for us today as it did for its original recipients? Why or why not?

4. When have you experienced criticism, pushback, or persecution for being a prophetic truth-teller about a particular aspect of our culture? How did you respond?

Regardless of how you may *feel*, you belong to a kingdom of God's possession. This kingdom isn't limited to a geographic location, and the power of the kingdom isn't limited to certain borders. The power of the kingdom resides in you. Jesus, through the power of the Holy Spirit, is exercising His kingly rule through you. Not just through good preachers, authors, or blue check mark Christians. Through *you*. I wonder if you've seen this beautiful and glorious responsibility yet. There are no spectators in God's kingdom. He has uniquely wired and uniquely placed you for His glory.[6]

5. What does it mean to you that the power of God's kingdom resides in you? How does Jesus exercise His kingly rule through you and your life?

PRAY | End your time in prayer. Thank God for His willingness to communicate His standards and guidelines for how you can know Him and should live your life for Him. Ask for continued insight and wisdom from the Holy Spirit as you go deeper into the book of Revelation.

APOCALYPSE NOW

The word *apocalypse* has become more mainstream in recent years. Based on its current usage, you might assume it means destruction, chaos, anarchy, or the end of the world. For this reason, it's important to consider what apocalyptic literature was actually about.

The English word *apocalypse* comes from the Greek *apokalypsis*, which literally means "uncovering" or "to take the cover off" of something.[7] By the Middle Ages—largely based on its usage in Revelation in reference to the second coming of Christ—the term *apocalypse* came to mean any kind of uncovering or unveiling, usually of a future event. By the late nineteenth century, the term *apocalypse* came to refer to disaster, chaos, and cataclysm— again based in part on John's symbolic and vivid description of Christ's return.[8]

However, in studying Revelation, it is important to remember the original Greek meaning of the word was "uncovering." If this is the case, it leads to the question of what has been *covered* and what is now being *revealed*. John states that his revelation, or *apocalypse*, is to reveal what "God gave [Jesus Christ] to show his servants what must soon take place" (Revelation 1:1). John thus wrote this letter to uncover this divinely inspired vision.

Similar to the way dreams contain surreal elements that require interpretation, apocalyptic literature uses vivid imagery, natural symbols, and unexpected contrasts to stir the readers' imaginations. Apocalyptic writing wants to engage its readers with more than just an intellectual understanding of ideas. As a result, it is not uncommon in apocalyptic literature to find people, places, and objects depicted as animals and natural phenomena and described symbolically with colors and numbers. These scenes thus may not conform to reality as you know it, as they are intended to provoke you to feel deeply and not just to grasp cognitively.

The book of Revelation reveals to believers in Christ that things are not always as they seem, both now and in the future. This message for Christians in the first century still applies to believers today. You are reminded—just as they were—that in spite of the sensory data you experience in the world around you, there is a lot more going on. God is still in control, Christ has secured your freedom, and a victorious future awaits you.

READ | Revelation 1:9–19; Isaiah 6:1–8; Joel 1:1–12

REFLECT

1. What has been your understanding or definition of *apocalypse* prior to this study? What has influenced your understanding of it up to this point?

2. Based on the description of apocalyptic literature, what elements do you recognize in Revelation 1:9–20? What image or symbol stands out in this passage?

Apocalyptic literature, in particular, tries to do things that seem strange to us. We're not image-heavy people in regard to how we learn. We're fact-heavy people, which is why we struggle to grapple with the strange pictures and images in books like Revelation. Even John has to ask the angel showing him the images, "What is that?" or "Who are they?" In apocalyptic literature, people are often represented in the likeness of animals, and historical events are represented in the form of natural phenomena, like earthquakes or floods. Colors and numbers have meaning. This means Revelation, like parts of Ezekiel, Daniel, Isaiah, Zechariah, and Joel, is full of imagery meant to inform our minds and ignite our spirits.[9]

3. Why is it important to remember that *apocalypse* literally means "unveiling" or "uncovering" rather than disaster, chaos, and cataclysmic events?

4. What similarities do you see between Revelation 1:9–20 and Isaiah 6:1–8? How do each of these passages shown an "unveiling" God's message to His people through His prophet?

Another reason God uses symbols and pictures in Revelation goes back to a rhythm we see throughout the Scriptures of God clearly making Himself known through teachings and commandments and then moving to pictures and symbols as judgment when people begin to scoff and mock. The symbols and pictures draw in believers while turning over scoffers and mockers to their folly.[10]

5. How do symbols and images speak to you differently than words? What impact do they have, particularly when referring to God, that language does not?

PRAY | End your time in prayer. Ask the Holy Spirit to help you understand the images and symbols found in the apocalyptic book of Revelation. Thank the Lord for creating you with imagination, creativity, and emotions so that you can understand Him and His messages in ways that go beyond mere knowledge, facts, and data.

CONNECT & DISCUSS

Take time today to connect with a group member and talk about some of the insights from this session. Use any of the prompts below to help guide your discussion.

What is one new thing you learned this week about the book of Revelation?

Which of the three literary "lenses" helped you approach Revelation with fresh eyes—as a letter, as prophecy, or as apocalypse? Why?

What is one personal reason you have for wanting to understand the meaning and message found in Revelation?

What does apocalyptic literature have in common with myths and fairy tales? How is it significantly different?

How would understanding the message of Revelation strengthen your faith?

CATCH UP & READ AHEAD

Use this time to go back and complete any of the study and reflection questions from previous days that you weren't able to finish. Make a note below of any questions you've had and reflect on any growth or personal insights you've gained.

Read Revelation 4-5 and review chapters 3-4 in *The Overcomers* before the next group session. Use the space below to make note of anything that stands out to you or encourages you.

WEEK 2

BEFORE GROUP MEETING	Read Revelation 4–5 Review chapters 3–4 in *The Overcomers* Read the Welcome section (page 22)
GROUP MEETING	Discuss the Connect questions Watch the video teaching for session 2 Discuss the questions that follow as a group Do the closing exercise and pray (pages 23–26)
STUDY 1	Complete the personal study (pages 29–31)
STUDY 2	Complete the personal study (pages 32–34)
STUDY 3	Complete the personal study (pages 35–37)
CONNECT & DISCUSS	Connect with someone in your group (page 38)
CATCH UP AND READ AHEAD (BEFORE WEEK 3 GROUP MEETING)	Read Revelation 6–7 Review chapter 5 in *The Overcomers* Complete any unfinished personal studies (page 39)

YOUR ULTIMATE REALITY

"You are worthy, our Lord and God, to receive glory and honor and power, for you created all things, and by your will they were created and have their being."

REVELATION 4:11

WELCOME | READ ON YOUR OWN

We have all witnessed events that we likely never imagined happening in our lifetimes. The impact of the Covid-19 pandemic alone left many of us reeling. We were forced to face shifting protocols that affected our families, communities, churches, and workplaces. Our world changed daily, requiring us to make decisions that we didn't see coming.

Trying to anticipate what would happen next left us feeling fearful, anxious, edgy, and exhausted. Although things have settled down a bit, we still experience wars abroad, divisive political landscapes, and the economic impact of constant change. We may also be dealing with physical limitations, addictive behaviors, and financial challenges. The ongoing barrage of these events can stretch our faith and gnaw at our hope.

The book of Revelation offers a calm heavenly eye in the midst of these storms of life. John, having addressed the problems faced by each of the seven churches (see Revelation 2–3), now relates a scene that has the power to reinforce our faith and alleviate our concerns. He reveals, "At once I was in the Spirit, and there before me was a throne in heaven with someone sitting on it" (4:2). John describes the One on the throne as translucent and bright, surrounded by vibrant colors and brilliant light, with a dazzling radiance.

In relating this vision to us, God wants us to see beyond our physical senses and earthly circumstances to realize the ultimate reality that is at the center of eternity. God was, is, and always will be on His throne. No matter what happens on earth, or how much the world seems to be unraveling, or how dramatically things are changing, we can rest assured that God is still on His throne and is worthy of our worship.

CONNECT | 15 MINUTES

If you or any of your group members don't know each other, take a few minutes to introduce yourselves. Then discuss one or both of the following questions:

- What is something that spoke to your heart in last week's personal study that you would like to share with the group?

— or —

- How do you generally view big changes in your life? Do you tend to dread and avoid them or anticipate and embrace them?

WATCH | 20 MINUTES

Read Revelation 4–5 before you watch the video teaching. Below is an outline of the key points. Note any questions or key concepts that stand out to you.

OUTLINE

I. The center of ultimate reality is revealed in Revelation 4–5 through a glimpse of heaven.
   A. John uses imagery designed to help us see what he experienced in the Spirit.
   B. Someone on a throne, which is described as dazzling and radiant, is at the center of this scene (see 4:2).
   C. All attention, affection, and worship are directed toward the throne and its occupant.

II. This throne-room scene summarizes the activity of God on earth and depicts God as one who moves toward us.
   A. God is the Creator, and all of creation—human and nonhuman—worships Him.
   B. The twenty-four elders (see 4:4) represent the twelve tribes of Israel (Old Testament) and the twelve apostles of Jesus (New Testament).
   C. The four creatures (see 4:6–7) represent God's creation and its fullness: the noblest (lion), the strongest (ox), the wisest (human), and the swiftest (eagle).

III. In addition to being the Creator, God is also seen as the Redeemer.
   A. Jesus—as the Lion of Judah, Root of David, and Lamb of God—redeems us.
   B. No one else can open the scroll—only Christ, the Lamb and the Lion.
   C. All heavenly hosts, beings we might be tempted to worship, fall down and worship the triumphant Christ.

IV. No matter what is going on in the world and/or in our lives, God is on the throne.
   A. This picture empowers us with joy and peace, captivating and inviting us into God's heart and His plans.
   B. Within the context of this place, we are seen for what and who we really are.
   C. This scene reminds us of the ultimate reality in heaven that never changes, no matter how much things change on earth.

V. John connects the church's worship to what is happening in the throne room, revealing a convergent space in which heaven and earth overlap.
   A. Our weariness in the midst of life's ups and downs can leave us feeling stuck in place.
   B. When we feel this way, we may lose sight of the only One who can open the scroll: Jesus.
   C. The scroll represents the preaching of Christ crucified on the cross to pay for our sins. He alone can open the scroll.

NOTES

DISCUSS | 35 MINUTES

Now discuss what you just watched by answering the following questions.

1. What are some of the details that stand out to you in the scene that John describes in Revelation 4–5? What do these particular details reveal about who God is?

2. Why is it important to remember that John relies on *language* to convey a scene that actually transcends human reality? How do the images and details of this throne-room scene speak directly to your imagination?

3. How does this scene that John describes in Revelation 4–5 comfort and reassure you in the midst of current world events and your own personal circumstances? Why does it comfort and reassure you in that way?

4. In John's vision, a mighty angel proclaimed, "Who is worthy to break the seals and open the scroll?" (Revelation 5:2). John wept when he heard this, "because no one was found who was worthy to open the scroll or look inside" (verse 4). When have you similarly felt stuck because you could not imagine how God was at work in your circumstances?

5. When Jesus opened the scroll, John heard angels "numbering thousands upon thousands, and ten thousand times ten thousand" (5:11). They encircled the throne and proclaimed, "Worthy is the Lamb, who was slain, to receive power and wealth and wisdom and strength and honor and glory and praise!" (verse 12). How does knowing that Jesus has done what no one else could do bolster your faith? How could focusing on Jesus and what He has done lead you to worship and praise Him in the midst of life's uncertainties and disappointments?

RESPOND | 10 MINUTES

Life's ups and downs can leave you feeling disappointed, desperate, and doubtful. At such times, you can weep just as John wept and refocus on the ultimate reality revealed in this scene in Revelation 4-5. No matter what you are experiencing, or how chaotic life seems to be, you can re-center your faith by focusing on what Jesus, the Lamb who was slain, has done for you. As you consider the incredible sacrifice He made to save you from sin and provide for you an eternal home, you can worship and praise Him regardless of your tumultuous circumstances. Use the questions below to help you reflect on this reassuring gift from God.

What is one concern, worry, or fear you have right now that is distracting you from focusing on the ultimate reality that John reveals in Revelation 4-5?

How does shifting your focus to what Jesus has done for you on the cross restore your perspective?

How can worshiping the Lamb before His throne strengthen your faith during challenging times?

PRAY | 10 MINUTES

End your time by praying together as a group. As you pray, ask the Holy Spirit to take you to God's radiant throne room and to help you see the ultimate reality John describes in his vision. Allow the truth of Jesus' atoning sacrifice to soothe your restless mind and troubled heart. Ask if anyone has prayer requests, and then write down those requests so that you and other group members can continue to pray about them in the week ahead.

PERSONAL STUDY

As you learned in this week's group time, your ultimate reality—that God is on His throne and Jesus has sacrificed Himself for you—is your anchor during difficult times and unexpected events. The scene described in Revelation 4-5 provides strength, hope, and joy no matter what else you might be feeling or experiencing. This week, you have the opportunity to conduct a spiritual checkup and explore two of the ongoing benefits of focusing on this ultimate reality—joy in tribulation and the power of worship. As you work through the exercises, be sure to write down your responses to the questions, as you will be given an opportunity to share your insights at the start of the next session if you are doing this study with others. If you are reading *The Overcomers* alongside this study, first review chapters 3-4 in the book.

SPIRITUAL CHECKUP

Annual checkups, with a physical exam and a battery of medical tests, become the norm as we grow older. These health assessments are not always pleasant for us, but they do provide an opportunity for a doctor to evaluate our physical health and, if needed, prescribe treatment or instruct us on how to make certain lifestyle adjustments. Conducting *spiritual* checkups on a regular basis is just as important to ensure the health of our relationship with God.

We saw a powerful example of such an assessment in Revelation 2–3. In those chapters, Jesus instructed John to write letters to seven churches in Asia Minor, giving each a direct assessment about the state of their congregation's spiritual health. When we come to Revelation 4, we get a glimpse of why Jesus desires His people to make these lifestyle changes. John sees God on His throne in heaven, surrounded by four living creatures who cry out, "'Holy, holy, holy is the Lord God Almighty,' who was, and is, and is to come" (verse 8).

Jesus desires for His followers to lead holy lives. In fact, He once instructed, "Be perfect, therefore, as your heavenly Father is perfect" (Matthew 5:48). Jesus is preparing an eternal home for those who remain faithful and true to Him (see John 14:3). So, just like any good doctor, He prescribes certain "treatments" to help us stay on course with our spiritual health. As Paul wrote, He helps us "run in such a way as to get the prize" (1 Corinthians 9:24).

Of course, this kind of spiritual checkup is not only about *you* or ensuring that you are at your healthiest. The body of Christ—the church—is made up of individuals who come together, love one another, and serve each other as they spread the gospel and advance God's kingdom. Knowing what health and vibrancy look like, and what sickness and death look like, prepares you to encourage and minister to others. When you are spiritually healthy, it allows you to pour into the lives of others and contribute to their spiritual health.

READ | Mark 2:13–17; Matthew 19:16–22; 1 Corinthians 9:24-27

REFLECT

1. In Mark 2:13–17, Jesus called Levi (also known as Matthew) to become His disciple. Levi then invited Jesus to a dinner where many "tax collectors and sinners" were present. How did the religious leaders respond to this? What did Jesus say He had come to do?

2. Jesus often provided spiritual checkups to those who were seeking to follow after God. In Matthew 19:16–22, what "treatment" did Jesus prescribe to the man who wanted eternal life? What did Jesus identify that was getting in the way of the man's relationship with God?

The last few years have made many feel like the universe is random and chaotic. I know it has felt like that to me. Trying to navigate the constant waves of tragedy, danger, and political turmoil while trying to serve my family in these anxious times, lead the church I pastor, and be a good friend has left me wondering, *What's next?* I can only imagine what things have been like for you. In Revelation 4–5, God is trying to put new lenses on our tired eyes: there is Someone on the throne.[11]

3. Jesus is not only the Great Physician but also the ruler over all creation (see Matthew 28:18). How does it help you to know that Jesus is in control today? What impact should this have on you as His follower when He instructs you to make a course correction in your life?

4. In 1 Corinthians 9:24–27, what does Paul say should be the focus of the "race" that Christians run? What type of training does he recommend to reach this goal?

For years I've taught, preached, and written that Christians need to know what stirs their affections for Jesus. Yes, singing, yes, the Scriptures, yes, community, but what else? The Holy Spirit tends to meet me outside and in the quiet. My affections are stirred by early mornings and a great cup of coffee. My heart will rejoice in the Lord when I can feast with a group of close friends.[12]

5. Is there anything that is robbing you of your affection for Jesus or distracting you from His beauty and majesty? If so, what changes can you implement to add more of what stirs your affection for Jesus and to eliminate what robs you of it?

PRAY | End your time in prayer. Ask God to reveal any spiritual health concerns to you. Thank Him for the ways that He continues to work in your life and draw you closer to Him.

JOY IN TRIBULATION

When we consider Jesus' messages to the seven churches of Revelation, only the congregations in Smyrna and Philadelphia were pictures of health. These two churches were healthy because of their love, commitment, and singlemindedness in following Jesus, *regardless of the cost*. Jesus told Smyrna to "not be afraid of what you are about to suffer" (Revelation 2:10). He said to Philadelphia, "The one who is victorious I will make a pillar in the temple of my God" (3:12).

The message from Jesus to these churches was not to fear the trials that were going to come but to persevere through them—drawing on His strength—and be victorious in the kingdom of God. Clearly, times of tribulation are not just things that will happen in the last couple of decades before Jesus returns. They have marked the church age from the beginning (the coming of Jesus) and will to the end (His return).

The apostles of the early church did not shy away from the fact that followers of Christ *will* face trials. Peter wrote, "Do not be surprised at the fiery ordeal that has come on you to test you" (1 Peter 4:12). Paul reminded us, "Our present sufferings are not worth comparing with the glory that will be revealed in us" (Romans 8:18)—a statement that indicates we will have present sufferings.

James made an even more surprising statement about trials: "Consider it pure joy, my brothers and sisters, whenever you face trials of many kinds, because you know that the testing of your faith produces perseverance" (James 1:2-3). His words may seem counterintuitive. How can we consider it pure *joy* when we face trials? The answer comes in knowing that facing trials, and persevering through them, builds our trust and faith in Christ. It also comes from knowing that God is on His throne, as we see in John's vision of heaven in Revelation 4-5.

When we focus on Jesus, what He has done, and the eternal home He has for us, it enables us to agree with Paul that our present struggles are "light and momentary" (2 Corinthians 4:17). We take joy in the fact that our trials have a purpose. And we look forward to the day when we will be with Christ and all our trials will be at an end.

READ | Acts 16:16-34; James 1:2-8; Hebrews 10:19-25

REFLECT

1. Paul devoted his life to spreading the gospel, but that didn't make him immune from experiencing trials. What situation, according to Acts 16:16–25, led to him and Silas being thrown in prison? What did the two men do when they were there?

2. What impact did Paul and Silas have on the jailer? What impact do you think you have on others when you are joyful and worship God in the midst of trials?

A few summers ago, we were on a family vacation at the beach. Lauren set up on the shore with a chair, umbrella, and book, while the kids and I ran into the water to take advantage of some good-size waves. We had a few boogie boards and got some pretty epic rides in. Every ten to fifteen minutes, I'd look to the shore to find Lauren, only to be unable to find her. In just ten to fifteen minutes, the currents had swept us far enough down the shoreline that I'd completely lost sight of her. This is what happens if we're not careful. The winds and waves of this fallen world will pull us along without us hardly feeling it, and we will look up and no longer be able to find where we started.[13]

3. When was the last time you were tempted to compromise rather than endure rejection (trials) from others because of your faith? What is the danger in making such compromises?

4. What does James say are the benefits of enduring trials? What is the "wisdom" you should request from God when you find yourself in the midst of tribulations (see James 1:2–8)?

Why must we fight to focus our attention on Jesus' reign and rule over and above everything else? If not, we will drift. We'll gather around smaller, weaker thrones, and we'll despair, lose heart, and fade. God has more for you. He sees you, loves you, hasn't abandoned you, and calls you back out to where the action is. You aren't meant to be a spectator in this great drama. That's what our enemy wants. He wants you to stay on the sideline, giving all you're attention to your weakness or the strength of your enemies. He wants you to be afraid and quiet. And he's put a whipping on a lot of us lately.[14]

5. The author of Hebrews states that Jesus has opened a way for you to enter into God's presence. He doesn't intend for you to just be a spectator in His grand drama. How does this encourage you and give you hope today? What are some ways you can come alongside those who are experiencing trials and help to "spur" them on (see Hebrews 10:19–25)?

PRAY | End your time in prayer. Ask God to empower you to remain focused on Jesus and His throne as you encounter life's problems, challenges, disappointments, and crises. Open your heart to the constant joy that is possible when Christ is your ultimate reality.

YOUR PLACE OF WORSHIP

In Revelation 4–5, we are invited into the ultimate reality of heaven—into an eternal place of worship. There, we see that the throne's occupant, "the Lord God Almighty" (4:8), is magnificent and gleaming, spotlighted by vibrant colors and brilliant light. His power, beauty, and majesty command complete attention and evoke terrifying awe.

In God's right hand is a scroll (see 5:1). The contents of the scroll represent God's plan of salvation and judgment—the purpose of human history, our stories, and how to make sense of all the pain we see and experience. In John's day, scrolls were sealed with wax and impressed with a signet ring to protect the contents and guarantee the message was from the originator. Only the owner of the scroll could open the seal and reveal its contents.[15]

This led to a problem. John stated, "No one in heaven or on earth or under the earth could open the scroll or even look inside it" (verse 3). In other words, no one had the authority and virtue for the task. This caused John to weep and weep (see verse 4). His sorrow was not lifted until one of the elders said that Jesus, "the Lion of the tribe of Judah, the Root of David" (verse 5), was able to open the scroll and break its seals.

The scene speaks to Jesus' authority to unseal the events in God's plan that will culminate in the kingdom reign of the Messiah. But it also speaks to our inability to make sense of everything we see going on in this world if we fail to keep our focus on God's throne. Like the Israelites wandering in the desert on their way to the promised land, we can get impatient and create tangible idols. Ours may not be a golden calf, but we are still prone to set up our own little thrones and seek from them what only the One on heaven's throne can provide.

Jesus unlocks the meaning of history. He brings salvation and judgment to the world. He administers mercy, justice, forgiveness, and redemption. He brings holiness, righteousness, wrath, and peace. Jesus brings everything into focus. This is why our eyes need to stay fixed on Him. If we lose sight of Him, we will drift. We will gather around smaller, weaker thrones, and we will despair, lose heart, and fade. Jesus alone is worthy of our worship.

READ | Deuteronomy 6:13–19; 1 Chronicles 16:23–30; 1 Timothy 1:12–17

REFLECT

1. What warning did Moses give to the Israelites in Deuteronomy 6:13–19? What was the promise if they did what was "right and good in the LORD's sight"?

Revelation 4 and 5 shows us what's happening underneath everything that exists. The Spirit is showing every Christian across human history, including you and me right now, that this isn't a future reality but a present one. You and I aren't waiting to die to go here. This isn't harps and wings and sitting on a cloud. This is the ultimate reality, and we've been invited in right now. This throne room right now, these creatures right now, everything seen and unseen right now, is in affection and attention pointed in this direction.[16]

2. The throne room of God in John's vision is not a *future* reality but a *present* one. What impact does it have on you when you consider that God is inviting you into this present reality?

3. Only the Lord is worthy of praise, honor, and respect (see 1 Chronicles 16:23–30). What are some of the idols and earthly thrones you have worshiped at times in your life? How did those idols and thrones disappoint you and leave you unsatisfied?

> When Jesus came, He opened up the heavens and brought the kingdom into all our spaces. There's a portal open, and goodness, beauty, and light are pouring in. That portal is you. You and I and all Christ followers are the place where goodness, beauty, and light emanate. That's why we need not shrink back or stay on the sidelines! The presence and power of Jesus is available to you at all times, and you are now an alien and a stranger in this present darkness.[17]

4. How do you see the kingdom of God operating in your life at this very moment? How are you a "portal" of His goodness, beauty, and light to others?

5. Paul understood how the power of God's kingdom could change a person's life. What was his condition before meeting Christ? How had Jesus changed him (see 1 Timothy 1:12–17)?

PRAY | End your time in prayer. Spend a few moments worshiping God for who He is and praising Him for all that He has done in your life. Confess any earthly thrones you have been worshiping and accept the forgiveness and mercy that Jesus extends to you.

CONNECT & DISCUSS

Take time today to connect with a group member and talk about some of the insights from this session. Use any of the prompts below to help guide your discussion.

What is one thing that stood out this week about who God is? About who Jesus is?

Which passage of Scripture most resonated with something you are facing?

What did you learn about the importance of worshiping God as a way to focus on ultimate reality?

How did this week's study make you rethink the way you go about your daily life?

What will you change in your life as a result of this week's study?

CATCH UP & READ AHEAD

Use this time to go back and complete any of the study and reflection questions from previous days that you weren't able to finish. Make a note below of any questions you've had and reflect on any growth or personal insights you've gained.

Read Revelation 6–7 and review chapter 5 in *The Overcomers* before the next group session. Use the space below to make note of anything that stands out to you or encourages you.

WEEK 3

BEFORE GROUP MEETING	Read Revelation 6–7
	Review chapter 5 in *The Overcomers*
	Read the Welcome section (page 42)
GROUP MEETING	Discuss the Connect questions
	Watch the video teaching for session 3
	Discuss the questions that follow as a group
	Do the closing exercise and pray (pages 42–46)
STUDY 1	Complete the personal study (pages 49–51)
STUDY 2	Complete the personal study (pages 52–54)
STUDY 3	Complete the personal study (pages 55–57)
CONNECT & DISCUSS	Connect with someone in your group (page 58)
CATCH UP AND READ AHEAD (BEFORE WEEK 4 GROUP MEETING)	Read Revelation 8–11
	Review chapter 6 in *The Overcomers*
	Complete any unfinished personal studies (page 59)

YOUR STRENGTH IN CHRIST

"For the Lamb at the center of the throne will be their shepherd; 'he will lead them to springs of living water. And God will wipe away every tear from their eyes.'"

REVELATION 7:17

WELCOME | READ ON YOUR OWN

"Origin stories" in books and movies reveal the events that have shaped a main character's identity. You learn about the losses, discoveries, failures, and successes that shaped the character's personality. You uncover why they are so vengeful, pessimistic, optimistic, or courageous. *You also* have an origin story as a follower of Jesus. Sometimes, these backstories are called your "testimony"—a summary that recounts how you came to know Christ and accept His gift of salvation. It is important to remember your particular origin story, because it helps you understand how God was at work in your life long before you made the decision to accept Jesus as your Savior.

Every person who makes up your family of faith has a similar backstory. They were once outside the kingdom of God but reached a point when they chose to be born again and were accepted into God's family through the life, death, and resurrection of Jesus. Traced back far enough, your origin story stretches all the way back to the day of Pentecost, when the early Jewish believers were filled with the Holy Spirit after Jesus' ascension (see Acts 1:16).

How did the gospel spread from those first followers to the more than two billion believers we see today? The answer can be found in Revelation 6–8. These scenes described by John uncover a different way to view your origin story . . . one that includes the obstacles and antagonists that virtually all believers have had to overcome for God's kingdom to endure. If you want to experience the full benefit of the reassurance that the book of Revelation provides—if you want to know who you really are as an *Overcomer*—then you need to know this part of the story.

CONNECT | 15 MINUTES

Get the session started by choosing one or both of the following questions to discuss together as a group:

- What is something that spoke to your heart in last week's personal study that you would like to share with the group?

— or —

- How would you title your Christian "origin story"? What three words best describe how you came to know Jesus?

WATCH | 20 MINUTES

Read Revelation 6–7 before you watch the video teaching. Below is an outline of the key points. Note any questions or key concepts that stand out to you.

OUTLINE

I. Revelation 6–7 reveals the major players fundamentally responsible for the pain and suffering in the world throughout history, beginning with the white horse, also known as the Antichrist.

   A. The white horse imitates the spiritual authority of Jesus and resembles many aspects of Christ (see 6:2).

   B. Outside the church, the white horse perpetuates self-actualization, the gospel of health and wellness, and subjective truth.

   C. Within the church, the white horse sows heresies, often by promoting extreme, yet unbalanced, versions of biblical truth.

II. The red horse represents war, violence, and human power struggles (see 6:4).

   A. War is woven into us and we are given over to it early and often in our lives.

   B. War, whether between tribes, nations, world powers, or individuals, is bloody and cruel, making life miserable and horrible.

   C. The red horse keeps the possibility of war present because anger resides in our hearts.

III. The black horse represents famine—not just lack of food, but lack of what we need most.

   A. Famine proclaims starvation rations can be had on minimum wages (see 6:6).

   B. Famine contrasts starvation rations with oil and wine, luxury items in the first century.

   C. The comparison reveals how the necessities of life go unmet amid the abundance of luxuries. We can have everything we think we want but at the expense of what we truly need.

IV. The pale horse represents pestilence, disease, and sickness unto death (see 6:8).

   A. The word for *pale* here denotes a yellowish green—the color of life-threatening illness.

   B. The sickness and pestilence of the pale horse mocks our medical innovations.

   C. Hades follows—sickness and fear, and the chaos that it causes.

V. In the face of these four horsemen, along with religious persecution (6:9–11) and natural catastrophe (6:12–17), everyone suffers and asks, "Who can stand?"

   A. Kings and great ones cannot stand, nor can generals and those in power. Rich and poor alike are not immune to suffering (6:15–16).

   B. Next, the servants of God are sealed—12,000 for each of the twelve tribes of Israel for a total of 144,000, a number of completeness and wholeness (7:4).

   C. The people of God are the ones who can stand—a countless multitude in white robes proclaiming, "Salvation belongs to our God, who sits on the throne, and to the Lamb" (7:9–10).

NOTES

DISCUSS | 35 MINUTES

Now discuss what you just watched by answering the following questions.

1. What associations and assumptions, either culturally or personally, have you had regarding the four horsemen in Revelation 6? How do you view them now after reading John's description?

2. In John's vision, he sees Jesus open the first through the fourth seals. What do each of the horsemen that are released symbolize? What is significant about the color of their horses?

3. Considering what the four horsemen symbolize, which of them seems to be the most predominant in wreaking destruction in the world today?

4. What are some of the obstacles, barriers, opponents, and circumstances you have overcome in your faith? How many of these are represented in Revelation 6–7?

5. Why are the people of God the only ones capable of standing in the face of false teaching, war, spiritual famine, disease, persecution, and natural catastrophes? How is the source of your power as a believer different than that of kings, great ones, generals, and the wealthy?

RESPOND | 10 MINUTES

It is important to remember that the four horsemen in John's vision had significance and relevance for the original recipients of his letter. They are not just part of some future event. John's original readers knew what it meant to endure false messiahs, wars, famines, diseases, persecution, and natural catastrophes. Also, keep in mind that John doesn't say anything in Revelation that hasn't already been said elsewhere in Scripture. For example, this passage follows the same order of Jesus' warnings in Matthew 24 about the last days in which we are still living.

Why is it important to remember that the scenes in Revelation 6–7 have significance and relevance to believers today?

What do you feel as you consider the impact the four horsemen have had on humankind throughout history?

How does focusing on the strength you have in Jesus impact any fears, worries, concerns, or apprehensions you have about the four horsemen and their impact?

PRAY | 10 MINUTES

End your time by praying together as a group. As you pray, ask God to help you understand the strength you have in Christ through the indwelling of the Holy Spirit. Acknowledge any fears, concerns, or lingering questions you may have—but also realize that God's power in you means you can endure, withstand, and overcome anything and everything represented by the four horsemen. Ask if anyone has prayer requests, and then write down those requests so that you and your fellow group members can continue to pray about them in the week ahead.

PERSONAL STUDY

As you learned this week, the opening of the seven seals and emergence of the four horsemen is a significant part of understanding who you are in Christ. The horsemen represent the power of deceit, death, division, depression, and disaster in this world. But God's people stand strong in the power of the Holy Spirit—the same Spirit that raised Jesus from the dead (see Romans 8:11). This week, you will explore what the Bible says about overcoming in the face of adversity and embracing suffering as an opportunity to draw closer to God. As you work through the exercises, write down your responses to the questions, as you will be given a few minutes to share your insights at the start of the next session if you are doing this study with others. If you are reading *The Overcomers* alongside this study, first review chapter 5 in the book.

HORSE SHOW

If you've ever been to a horse show, you know that judges base their criteria on appearance as well as performance. In Revelation 6, John presents us with a very different kind of horse show—one that displays terrifying symbols of all that is wrong with the world. The appearance of each of the four horses matters (primarily their color), as does the purpose of each rider.

The white horse and its rider appear regal and benign (see 6:2). But looks can be deceiving, for the rider represents an imitation Christ. The fiery red horse and its rider trample peace and bring bloodshed through anger and war (see verse 4). The black horse and its scale-bearing rider bring famine of heart, mind, and spirit—not just body (see verse 6). The pale horse bears Death as its rider, with Hades trailing behind them (see verse 8). While these may seem like mythic creatures straight out of a fantasy novel, they represent a particular destructive force—false teaching, war, famine, and death. These forces have galloped across the earth for centuries and trampled countless human lives. Their particular kind of destruction can be summed up as an abstract, but their impact on individual lives has always been personal.

If you find these four horsemen unsettling, you are not alone. What they represent has frightened and disrupted men and women for centuries. It is a natural human response. But such a reaction is also part of how God created you to survive. Your emotions signal that you need to take a protective stance—usually summed up as fight, flight, freeze, or feint.

Sometimes, you may think that experiencing fear or anxiety means your faith is weak. But that's not the case at all. It's what you *do* in response to your fears that determines their impact on your faith. Throughout the Bible, we frequently see men and women enduring the destruction, loss, and pain symbolized by the four horse-men. Most of them naturally experience fear at first and then realize they can draw on the strength of the Lord. You have the same choice every time the four horsemen gallop into your life. You can suffer them in your own power. Or you can overcome them through Christ's power in you.

READ | 2 Corinthians 12:6–10; John 16:32–33; Psalm 27:1–3

REFLECT

1. Which of the four horsemen evokes the most fear in you? Why do you think that particular horse and its rider hits so close to home?

2. It is easy to fall into the trap of thinking that experiencing fear or anxiety means that your faith is weak. What does Paul say about the weakness he experienced (see 2 Corinthians 12:6–10). What did his particular struggle help him realize about Christ's power?

God—in His sovereign reign over all things—holds all evil on a leash, including Satan, demons, and the brokenness that leads to sin and suffering. Nothing, not even the brokenness of the cosmos, is without boundaries and limits. Evil and suffering are not omnipotent. They don't have the final say or authority.[18]

3. How does it encourage you to know that God holds evil "on a leash"? What is a situation in your life where you need Him to demonstrate this reality to you?

4. Jesus knew that life would be difficult for His disciples after He left the earth. What did He say would happen to them? What were they to remember (see John 16:32–33)?

> The Scriptures don't seem to be interested in answering all our questions. In the last five chapters of the book of Job, we see there are things we, as finite, created beings, won't be able to comprehend that God, in His infinite power and wisdom, can. He is good. Look to Jesus. Watch Him as He reveals the kingdom of God.[19]

5. What did David say about his fears and God's goodness in Psalm 27:1–3? How can you follow David's example this week and rely on God in the face of all your fears?

PRAY | End your time in prayer. Ask God to remind you of the power dwelling in you through the Holy Spirit. Tell Him about your fears and concerns and then thank Him for making you an Overcomer who can withstand anything you encounter.

WORSE BEFORE BETTER

The breaking of the first four seals ushered in the arrival of the four horsemen—revealing to us the reality of false gospels, angry hearts, empty bellies and souls, and sickness of all kinds (see Revelation 6:1–8). With the opening of the fifth seal, we see that religious persecution often compounds the suffering of believers (see verses 9–11). When the sixth seal is opened, we are made aware of the fact that natural calamities, and all the destruction they bring on the earth, continually loom over us.

All of this paints a grim picture of life on earth. In truth, we all have borne witness to the devastating impact of pain and loss in this world. We experience disappointment and betrayal in our relationships. Injuries and disease impair our bodies and cause physical pain. Financial pressures, mounting debts, and unexpected expenses seem to crush us. Our faith feels put to the test, and we aren't sure how we can hold on.

During these "worse before better" times, we need to shift perspective and remind ourselves of who God is, dare and trust that He is always present with us, and believe that somehow He will make a way forward even when we cannot see one. When it comes to suffering, we know from the Bible that God isn't the author of evil but is the source of beauty, goodness, and truth. God is good (see Mark 10:18), all the works of His hands are faithful and just (see Psalm 111:7), and there is no darkness in Him at all (see 1 John 1:5).

Evil, suffering, and death are the result of sin and humankind's rebellion against their Creator. This isn't to say that everything we endure is our fault. The cosmos is fractured at both the macro and micro levels. Some suffering—maybe most suffering—flows from this reality. The cosmos is broken and does not function as it was designed.

Our hope for moving from worse to better in this broken world comes from recognizing that God can use what the enemy intended to harm us for His good purposes. God is sovereign over all things. He isn't the author of evil, yet when evil happens, He has the power to take the destructive impact of evil and redeem it for something positive in our lives.

READ | Genesis 50:15–21; Psalm 27:13–14; Philippians 4:4–7

REFLECT

1. Joseph's life was filled with trials—all of which began when he was betrayed by his brothers and sold into slavery. They had done a great evil against him. But what did Joseph recognize about the hand of God in everything that had happened (see Genesis 50:15–21)?

2. When was the last time you felt your faith stretched to the breaking point? What did you ultimately learn about God—and yourself—through the experience?

I don't want to soft-sell the tribulation and sorrow that's coming. These things are going to grow more fierce, not less, and we're going to see that in the years to come. . . . These riders have been unleashed on humankind, and we've steadily built anger and opposition. For what reason? Because the people of God are confronting evil all over the world, and the kingdom of God has spread despite their best shot. The four riders are getting more frantically angry because we're taking ground.[20]

3. What are some ways that you have confronted evil lately in your world? How have you pushed back against the destruction of the four horsemen?

4. The author of Psalm 27:13–14 expressed his confidence that he would see the goodness of the Lord in his life. How can such confidence in God's infinite goodness motivate you to exercise patience and wait on Him during challenging times?

For almost thirty years, I've watched as followers of Jesus have been diagnosed with illness, killed in tragic accidents, and been on the receiving end of terrible tragedies. Yet, in almost every case, the "peace that passes understanding" (Philippians 4:7) does its work, and those people begin to minister to others who are hurting. Where evil tried to destroy, God turned it on its head. He sovereignly redeems the suffering of His people by exposing idols, growing their faith and dependence, and granting them His presence in unique and beautiful ways.[21]

5. How has God redeemed something in your life that was intended to harm you? How have you experienced the peace of God that transcends understanding (see Philippians 4:4–7)?

PRAY | End your time in prayer. Bring your fears, concerns, worries, and burdens before God and trust that He hears you and cares about everything you now surrender to Him. Ask Him to redeem what continues to seem worse so that you can experience His better.

YOU'RE STILL STANDING

When we look at what John has described so far, we might wonder what we're supposed to find reassuring. We're there in God's heavenly throne room, and we're trained on His radiant presence, His almighty power, beauty, and sovereignty. But then we learn what will happen during this season of history: false prophets, wars and violence, spiritual and emotional starvation, sickness, and death. And there will also be some persecution and natural disasters along the way.

Under the weight of so much pain and brokenness, where is the encouragement? John answers that question for us in Revelation 7. Yes, it is true that when it comes to the four horsemen and all the strife and calamity in the world, no one is immune. No one escapes life without pain and suffering. No matter how powerful, accomplished, famous, attractive, smart, or rich a person might be, all are susceptible to these calamities.

So who *can* stand when the world turns upside down and our lives feel inside out? *You* can stand. You and all your fellow brothers and sisters in Christ.

In John's vision, he sees a multitude of believers gathered from every nation, tribe, and people group (see 7:9). These believers proclaim, "Salvation belongs to our God, who sits on the throne, and to the Lamb" (verse 10). After all they had been through, all they had suffered and endured, they were still standing because of the power of Jesus Christ.

The same is true of you. You've had loved ones get sick. You've experienced seasons where anger overwhelmed you or someone else's rage caused you harm. You've been betrayed by those who claimed to love you. You've suffered loss and defeat, insult and injury, haters and trolls. Yet you are still standing alongside every member of the body of Christ.

Who can stand in the face of Satan's evil? The church of Jesus can stand. You can stand against all the demonic forces that have been unleashed and still proclaim that Christ is King. God is good, and you are anchored in His presence, standing strong in the power of His Spirit.

READ | Ephesians 6:10–12; James 4:7–10; 1 Peter 5:8–11

REFLECT

1. Who does Paul state in Ephesians 6:10–12 is your true enemy in this world? What are you able to do each day if you put on the armor that God provides?

> So, when the question is asked, "Who can stand in light of the four riders? Who can stand in the ancillary sorrows of religious persecution and natural calamities?" Jesus' answer is, "My people can stand. And not only will they stand, but they'll sing in the face of the riders." We can see this throughout our history. When the sorrows and brokenness of the world befall the people of God, we tend to sing.[22]

2. What does it mean to "sing" in the presence of the riders, persecution, and natural calamities of this world? When have you "sang" in the midst of suffering?

3. According to James 4:7–10, what are you to do when the devil tries to attack you? What happens when you choose to draw near to God during such times?

> Here we stand in the midst of a wild and discombobulating time, singing our songs to Christ. This is our victory, and the four horsemen know it. They know we're closer, so you should expect, like whomping a wasp nest, for them to fly around and want to sting, and even as they sting during our run through this gauntlet, we'll sing in their faces.[23]

4. How does Peter describe your enemy in 1 Peter 5:8–11? What does he say that you can know about your fellow brothers and sisters in Christ as you stand firm?

5. *You are not alone!* Think about some of the people who have supported you during some of life's storms. How did those people reveal God's presence to you? How have you likewise been a source of strength to a fellow brother or sister in Jesus?

PRAY | End your time in prayer. Thank God for all that He has helped you overcome. Ask Him to give you confidence and strength to trust Him as you move forward each day.

CONNECT & DISCUSS

Take time today to connect with a group member and talk about some of the insights from this session. Use any of the prompts below to help guide your discussion.

What is one new thing you learned this week from Revelation 6–7?

What is one way this week's study challenged you to grow in your faith?

How does knowing you can withstand life's pain and chaos change the way you relate to others?

Which of the images or symbols from Revelation 6–7 stands out to you or lingers with you?

What verse or passage of Scripture from this week's personal studies means the most to you?

CATCH UP & READ AHEAD

Use this time to go back and complete any of the study and reflection questions from previous days that you weren't able to finish. Make a note below of any questions you've had and reflect on any growth or personal insights you've gained.

Read Revelation 8–11 and review chapter 6 in *The Overcomers* before the next group session. Use the space below to make note of anything that stands out to you or encourages you.

WEEK 4

BEFORE GROUP MEETING	Read Revelation 8–11 Review chapter 6 in *The Overcomers* Read the Welcome section (page 62)
GROUP MEETING	Discuss the Connect questions Watch the video teaching for session 4 Discuss the questions that follow as a group Do the closing exercise and pray (pages 62–66)
STUDY 1	Complete the personal study (pages 69–71)
STUDY 2	Complete the personal study (pages 72–74)
STUDY 3	Complete the personal study (pages 75–77)
CONNECT & DISCUSS	Connect with someone in your group (page 78)
CATCH UP AND READ AHEAD (BEFORE WEEK 5 GROUP MEETING)	Read Revelation 12–13 Review chapters 7–8 in *The Overcomers* Complete any unfinished personal studies (page 79)

YOUR WITNESS TO THE WORLD

"But in the days when the seventh angel is about to sound his trumpet, the mystery of God will be accomplished, just as he announced to his servants the prophets."

REVELATION 10:7

WELCOME | READ ON YOUR OWN

You don't have to surf social media very long to encounter *schadenfreude*. The term, derived from German, literally means "damage" or "harm" (*schaden*) and "joy" (*freude*).[24] It refers to a feeling of delight when someone gets their "just desserts" and suffers the consequences of their self-centered decisions and actions.

As followers of Jesus, we are called to a higher standard in how we respond to the misery suffered by others due to their mistakes or moral failures. Rather than offering a smug I-told-you-so righteousness, we are instructed to "mourn with those who mourn" (Romans 12:15) and to clothe ourselves "with compassion, kindness, humility, gentleness and patience" (Colossians 3:12).

Whenever humans turn their backs on God and elevate themselves to His status, it leads to devasting results for them, for others, and for creation. Those who receive God's wrath choose it by siding with the enemy rather than surrendering to the Lordship of Jesus. God has made a way for every person on the earth to be saved and experience life to the full (see John 3:16; Luke 19:10). But He allows us to choose.

Revelation 8–11 contains some of the most heartbreaking images in the Bible. The seven trumpets reveal the horrendous reality of those outside of Christ who cling to their idols . . . and who, consequently, suffer the power of demonic forces behind those idols. Curiously, these extraordinary images are meant to help us as believers love the world we are in. As Overcomers, we respect God's judgment as good and just while simultaneously lamenting the destruction that sin causes in the world.

CONNECT | 15 MINUTES

Get the session started by choosing one or both of the following questions to discuss together as a group:

- What is something that resonated with you in last week's personal study that you would like to share with the group?

— *or* —

- When have you experienced *schadenfreude* or been glad that someone seemed to get what they deserved?

WATCH | 20 MINUTES

Read Revelation 8–11 before you watch the video teaching. Below is an outline of the key points. Note any questions or key concepts that stand out to you.

OUTLINE

I. In Revelation 8–11, God uses the seven trumpets to unveil reality to those outside of Christ.
   A. Similar things happen in Exodus with the ten plagues, but the judgments here represent a complete devolution of the cosmos.
   B. God's judgment shows that He cares and our choices matter to Him (see 8:2–9:21).
   C. God's judgment is in response to the prayers of the martyrs.

II. The partial judgment of God on the earth represents His mercy.
   A. God allows evil to wreak havoc, but it results only in the partial destruction of the earth and humanity (see 8:7–13; 9:18).
   B. The demonic forces that stand behind our idols will enact war against the very people who worship them.
   C. Yet in spite of their horrific torment, unbelievers refuse to repent (see 9:20–21).

III. In the midst of God's judgment, the church is called to be a faithful witness (see 10:1–11:14).
   A. John is to warn unbelievers about judgment and call them to repent (see 10:1–11).
   B. John's eating of the scroll (see 10:9–11) symbolizes an internalization of the message he is called to give.
   C. Just as the scroll is both sweet and sour, the content of the prophecy contains both judgment and redemption (see 10:9–11).

IV. Gentiles will be allowed to persecute the church for a time (forty-two months), yet believers remain under God's protection (see 11:1–14).
   A. John's measuring of the temple communicates God's ownership and divine protection of His people (see Ezekiel 40–42; Zechariah 1:16).
   B. John is unable to measure the outer courts of the temple, which have been given over to the Gentiles.
   C. While the pagan empire will rise up against the church, the witness of martyrs will bring nations to repentance.

V. The seventh trumpet signals the culmination of God's redemptive plan (see 11:15–19).
   A. The kingdom of the world has become the kingdom of the Lord and Jesus the Messiah, who will reign forever (see 11:15).
   B. The time has come for judging the dead and rewarding God's servants (see 11:18).
   C. The Lord God Almighty, "who is and who was" (11:17), reigns with sovereign power.

NOTES

DISCUSS | 35 MINUTES

Now discuss what you just watched by answering the following questions.

1. God's wrath, judgment, and righteous anger are evidence of His love for His creation. Do you agree that love gets diluted and becomes weak without judgment and account-ability? How have you experienced this in one of your relationships with a loved one?

2. The trumpet judgments reveal that many people, in spite of facing the conse-quences of their idolatry, still refuse to repent and accept God's gift of salvation in Christ. Why do you think so many people resist repentance even when their idols cause them suffering?

3. When have you been able to show empathy for another person's suffering while calling him or her to change direction and move toward God? What were the results of your actions?

4. What are some of the ways that you see the church persecuted and denounced by unbelievers in your community? How does your response reflect God's love as well as His righteousness?

5. The seventh angel announced, "The kingdom of the world has become the kingdom of our Lord and of his Messiah" (Revelation 11:15). How does it encourage you to know that the church is victorious? How does it influence your interactions with nonbelievers?

RESPOND | 10 MINUTES

It's not easy to see other people suffer from their sinful choices, yet merely pointing out their wrongdoing rarely motivates them to change. Instead, we are called to be "salt" and "light" in the world (see Matthew 5:13–16). We are to lead by example . . . finding the balance between upholding God's standards of righteousness and showing His mercy. So much of how we communicate the gospel comes from our attitude and actions, not just our words! Just as John ate the sweet-tasting scroll only to have it sour in his stomach, so we are called to metabolize God's grace while knowing that others' rejection of it can cause us heartburn.

Do you find it easier to uphold God's standards of righteousness or extend His mercy to those who do not know Him? Explain your response.

How do you express love for people while making it clear you hate the sin in their lives?

How can you respond with the love of Christ the next time you are tempted by *schadenfreude* in response to someone's downfall?

PRAY | 10 MINUTES

End your time by praying together as a group. As you pray, ask God to help you hold the tension between His judgment and righteousness on one hand and His mercy and lovingkindness in the other. Ask if anyone has prayer requests, and then write down those requests so that you and your fellow group members can continue to pray about them in the week ahead.

PERSONAL STUDY

In this week's group time, you saw how God's wrath and judgment reflect His love and mercy. The seven trumpets in Revelation 8–11 reveal terrible scenes of destruction, as God allows unbelievers to experience the consequences of their idolatry. Believers suffer in the wake of persecution and calamity but ultimately remain protected because they have been sealed by the Holy Spirit. This week, you will explore how to balance God's judgment, mercy, wrath, and love in your own life and in your witness to the world. As you work through the exercises, be sure to write down your responses to the questions, as you will be given a few minutes to share your insights at the start of the next session if you are doing this study with others. If you are reading *The Overcomers* alongside this study, first review chapter 6 in the book.

JUNK DRAWER

In most homes, one drawer becomes a catchall for items that don't seem to have a place of their own. What's worth saving tends to be subjective, of course, and a junk drawer reflects an odd assortment of disparate parts, pieces, and remnants. You might find a couple loose AA batteries, a half-burned candle, some twine, used twist ties, rubber bands, salt-and-pepper packets, takeout menus, and freebie pens.

The way we define love today often resembles a junk drawer. It includes a little bit of everything . . . and thus ends up meaning nothing. People talk about loving burgers, their pets, and their hobbies in much the same way as they talk about loving their spouse, children, families, friends, God, local church, and country. Surely, all this love is not the same! The word *love* has been emptied of its meaning.

Further diluting the meaning of love, popular culture tends to define it as complete agreement, support, and affirmation. Tolerance is upheld and enforced, yet it only seems available to those who completely agree, support, and affirm our culture's fluid values. This belief harms those outside the church, but it also erodes the confidence of those inside the church because it is out of step with reality. Everyone suffers whenever we live in the confusion and absurdity of a make-believe world.

The truth is that the more we love something, the more capability we have for judgment and wrath to protect it. Think about this in terms of a parent-child relationship. Parents must judge what is helpful and harmful for their children. Parents must also protect their children from harm—and those who try to harm their children will feel the full extent of their wrath. This parental wrath is not fueled by hatred but is rooted in love for their children.

God, as a perfect heavenly Father, exemplifies this capacity for love perfectly. His love is expansive and infinite. Therefore, His wrath and judgment are righteous and immense. If we want to witness His love to those around us, then we must be prepared to take love out of its cultural junk drawer. Our love must have clarity, discernment, and accountability.

READ | 1 Corinthians 13:3–8; John 3:16–21; 1 John 4:9–10

REFLECT

1. Do you agree that the way our world defines love is similar to a junk drawer—a catchall for everything and anything? How have you noticed this in the way others use the word *love*?

2. How does Paul define love in 1 Corinthians 13:4–8? How is this similar to or different from the way that people in this world tend to define love?

> This is love made visible. Jesus has come that you and I might walk in the light, have souls that burst forth with living water, and have life to the full. In 1 John, the apostles argued that we can't define love by looking at humanity because all of our love is tainted by our sinfulness. All our definitions fall short. We have to start with God. He's untainted by sin and perfect in all His ways. This perfect love of God rooted in His character makes God ultimate in love but rightly capable of judgment and wrath.[25]

3. How would you describe the difference between human love and divine love? Why do all our definitions fall short when seen in the light of God's perfect love?

4. In John 3:16–21, we are told that God sent His Son into the world not to condemn it but to save it through Jesus' sacrifice on the cross. How does the fact that God sent Jesus to live, die, and rise again reflect both His righteousness as well as His mercy?

Love has been made visible. The scandal of the incarnation is that the Son of God, the second person of the Trinity—eternal and omnipotent—took on flesh and walked among us. The love of God was made manifest among us. The active agent in creating everything we see and know comes down and puts on flesh—comes as a baby. This love is playing out among us! This love has come so that you and I can live through Him.[26]

5. Why is the incarnation—Jesus taking on flesh and living among us—considered scandalous? What else do you learn from 1 John 4:9–10 about God's love for you?

PRAY | End your time in prayer. Bring any concerns or questions you have about God's love before Him. Ask Him to help you understand how His righteousness and wrath are necessary parts of His loving mercy.

AMERICAN IDOL

The book of Revelation makes it clear that the consequences of idolatry are far more sobering and dangerous than any reality TV competition. The winners of those programs are often chosen based on popularity and not necessarily on merit. Similarly, the idols that people choose to worship often reflect their own subjective perspective and not God's reality.

At one point in John's vision, he hears an angel proclaim that the trumpet blasts he is hearing are God's judgments for "the inhabitants of the earth" (Revelation 8:13). The phrase refers to those who stand in the way of God's coming kingdom—those who are in rebellion against the Lord.[27] Those who receive God's wrath choose it by siding with the enemy rather than surrendering to Jesus, for God has made a way for all people to be saved.

The judgments unleashed by the trumpets do not affect everyone. Although followers of Jesus—much like the Israelites in Egypt during the time of the ten plagues—may experience some of these judgments, they will be protected from the worst that come on the earth. We see this starting with the fifth trumpet, where the locusts are told not to harm those who belong to God: "They were told not to harm the grass of the earth or any plant or tree, but only those people who did not have the seal of God on their foreheads" (9:4).

What God is attempting to do through these judgments is get the attention of the unbelievers so they will repent and turn to Christ. He uses the plagues to reveal to these people that everything in which they are trusting—their sense of self, peace, comfort, and meaning—are idols that cannot save them. These idols, and the demonic powers behind them, gladly receive the worship of these people, only to turn and destroy them in the end.

God is thus exposing these idols of comfort and control for what they truly are. Yet in spite of this, we find the unbelievers doubling down on worshiping them instead of the one true God (see 9:20-21). They foolishly continue to reject the Creator of the universe, live in their own sinful ways, and put their hope in things that cannot save them.

READ | Romans 1:21-27; Psalm 107:10-16; 2 Peter 2:4-10

REFLECT

1. How does Paul describe those who choose idols over God (see Romans 1:21-23)? What does God do when people make this choice (see verses 24-27)?

2. How do you respond to the people in your life who have chosen idols over God? How do you set yourself apart and avoid temptation while continuing to show them God's love?

Man is proven dependent and helpless quickly when the things he needs to survive physically are taken from him. David Campbell stated, "Through the suffering, deprivation, and death continually occurring in history, unbelievers are confronted with the reminder that the world and their lives remain in the hands of God, and their idolatrous trust in things other than God has been gravely and fatally misplaced."[28] Where the earth groans and writhes under the curse of sin, subjected to futility, waiting on the redemption of the sons of God, people die and are maimed.[29]

3. What does the author of Psalm 107:10-16 say happens to those who choose to live in rebellion to God? What happens when they cry out to God for mercy?

4. How have you experienced this in your life? When is a time that God delivered you from a bad situation that had been brought about by your own sinful choices?

Do you trust in your body to save you? It's not going to happen. Trust your diet? Gone. Your bunker and your canned goods? Gone. Your stockpiled ammo? Gone. Your social media presence? Gone. The power of your stuff? Gone. This is the world's experience with demonization. They are tormented and tortured. As Overcomers, we aren't subject to this kind of torment because we've found our security in Jesus. We worship and pray, trust and repent, hope and lament, preach and fast. That doesn't mean that we can't experience certain levels of demonic oppression, just that the indwelling Holy Spirit saves us from the worst effects of these enemies of the world.[30]

5. Who does Peter say is subject to God's judgment (see 2 Peter 2:4–8)? What does Peter say about God's willingness to protect the godly in these judgments?

PRAY | End your time in prayer. Ask God to help you resist the pull of idols and the influence of unbelievers who worship them. Thank Him for His sovereignty and protection in your life.

SWEET AND SOUR

In Revelation 10, a voice from heaven speaks to John and tells him to "take the scroll that lies open in the hand of the angel" (verse 8). When John does this, the angel says, "Take it and eat it. It will turn your stomach sour, but 'in your mouth it will be as sweet as honey'" (verse 9). In this scene, the scroll represents the Word of God.[31] It is "sweet as honey" to those receive it, but "sour" in the sense that not everyone will receive it and will thus face God's judgment.

Just as John was instructed to eat the scroll presented to him, so we are called to share the sweet taste of God's grace and mercy with the world. Yet also like John, as we do this we mourn the fact that there will some who will reject God's offer of salvation. This should leave a sour taste in our mouths and motivate us to bring as many lost souls into God's kingdom as possible . . . while there still is time. As Jesus said, "As long as it is day, we must do the works of him who sent me. Night is coming, when no one can work" (John 9:4).

Jesus came into the world "to seek and to save the lost" (Luke 19:10). He came not "to condemn the world, but to save the world" (John 3:17). He calls all those who desire to follow after Him to likewise "go into all the world and preach the gospel to all creation" (Mark 16:15). As we do this, we become His heralds of the good news. As Paul wrote, "We are therefore Christ's ambassadors, as though God were making his appeal through us" (2 Corinthians 5:20).

This is why it is so imperative for you to believe that you were made for this day! You cannot shrink back from the spiritual battlefront. You cannot become a spectator on the sidelines. God has turned "the inhabitants of the earth" (Revelation 8:13) over to their own desires. He has given them what they want—and it's destroying them. As an Overcomer, your mission is to endure in the brokenness of this world and let others know there is a way out.

READ | Ezekiel 2:9–3:3; Matthew 5:13–16; Colossians 3:15–17

REFLECT

1. What similarities do you see between John 10:8–11 and Ezekiel 2:9–3:3? What are some of the differences you see between these passages?

2. How would you describe your relationships with those in your life who do not know Jesus? Are you strongly compelled to share the gospel with them?

> You and I live right in the middle of all this death, brokenness, and despair. We were made for this day, and this day for us. As Christians how should we live in light of the seven trumpets? [Jesus] says that you are the salt of the earth—the light of the world. Amid all this catastrophic loss, we are examples of repentance. We are called to pray for the world and herald the good news wherever God has placed us.[32]

3. What does it mean to be the "salt of the earth" and "light of the world" (see Matthew 5:13–16)? What happens when salt loses its flavor and light is hidden?

4. When was the last time an unbeliever noticed that you were a follower of Jesus? What caught their attention to signal that you were different from them?

Jesus has granted spiritual power to you. Jesus has given you a community to trust. Jesus has given you His Word to cling to. The world needs Christians that hate their sin and can be the living embodiment of peace in calamity. Overcomers are a stabilizing, unanxious presence amid moral decline and the world's chaos. Let's be people who continually throw ourselves on God's mercy in habitual confession and repentance.[33]

5. How does Paul say in Colossians 3:15–17 that believers are to react to the chaos of this world? How does your lifestyle of faith reflect the peace of Jesus to others?

PRAY | End your time in prayer. Ask God to give you a greater desire to see the lost come into His kingdom. Pray that He will use you as His ambassador for Christ in this world.

CONNECT & DISCUSS

Take time today to connect with a group member and talk about some of the insights from this session. Use any of the prompts below to help guide your discussion.

What stood out this week about how God can use you to draw others to Him?

What image, symbol, or trumpet stands out to you from this week's study? Why?

Who are the unbelievers you feel burdened to lift up in prayer in light of what you've learned?

What is one area in which you would like prayer so that you can grow stronger in your faith and in your testimony to others?

What is one thing you can do to bring peace to the calamity you see in other people's lives?

CATCH UP & READ AHEAD

Use this time to go back and complete any of the study and reflection questions from previous days that you weren't able to finish. Make a note below of any questions you've had and reflect on any growth or personal insights you've gained.

Read Revelation 12–13 and review chapters 7–8 in *The Overcomers* before the next group session. Use the space below to make note of anything that stands out to you or encourages you.

WEEK 5

BEFORE GROUP MEETING	Read Revelation 12–13 Review chapters 7–8 in *The Overcomers* Read the Welcome section (page 82)
GROUP MEETING	Discuss the Connect questions Watch the video teaching for session 5 Discuss the questions that follow as a group Do the closing exercise and pray (pages 82–86)
STUDY 1	Complete the personal study (pages 89–91)
STUDY 2	Complete the personal study (pages 92–94)
STUDY 3	Complete the personal study (pages 95–97)
CONNECT & DISCUSS	Connect with someone in your group (page 98)
CATCH UP AND READ AHEAD (BEFORE WEEK 6 GROUP MEETING)	Read Revelation 14–16 Review chapter 9 in *The Overcomers* Complete any unfinished personal studies (page 99)

YOUR ENEMY IN FOCUS

All inhabitants of the earth will worship the beast—all whose names have not been written in the Lamb's book of life, the Lamb who was slain from the creation of the world.

REVELATION 13:8

WELCOME | READ ON YOUR OWN

Most films depicting battle scenes—whether the forests of Middle Earth, the shores of Normandy, or a galaxy far, far away—typically have a moment when the camera pans away to show the enormity of the conflict. This shift in perspective allows the viewer to see the struggle as not between just a few combatants but as one that involves hundreds or thousands of participants.

The scene that John presents in Revelation 12–13 serves a similar purpose. Up to this point, we have been to heaven's throne room and gazed upon ultimate reality. Seals have been opened, revealing what the church can expect between the ascension of Christ and His second coming. We have seen how the trumpets illustrate the way in which unbelievers and believers will distinctly navigate the brokenness of this world.

Now, we are taken to an interlude—a vision of a woman who is confronted by a dragon. We then see two beasts: one who rises out the sea, and another who rises out of the earth. In this way, the perspective shifts to a wide lens so we can see our enemy in focus—defeated yet completely devoted to taking down God's people.

This shift in perspective enables us to catch a glimpse of the cosmic battle that is currently being waged—of Michael and his angels fighting against the dragon and his demonic host. In this way, we realize that we are *already* engaged in spiritual warfare. And as we become aware of these realities at work right now, we wake up and do our part as Overcomers.

CONNECT | 15 MINUTES

Get the session started by choosing one or both of the following questions to discuss together as a group:

- What is something that spoke to your heart in last week's personal study that you would like to share with the group?

  — *or* —

- What is your favorite movie depicting a war or battle scene? Do you prefer historical battles, science fiction scuffles, or superhero showdowns?

WATCH | 20 MINUTES

Read Revelation 12–13 before you watch the video teaching. Below is an outline of the key points. Note any questions or key concepts that stand out to you.

OUTLINE

I. Revelation 12–13 reveals the cosmic war between the enemy and God's people.
   A. Revelation 12 opens with a woman and uses imagery from Genesis 37:9.
   B. Another Old Testament reference, Isaiah 66:7–9, implies the woman to be the nation of Israel.
   C. The woman represents the people of God. She is Israel, Mary, and the ideal church in heaven all at once.

II. Next, the great dragon, representing Satan, emerges to emphasize the cosmic war with a defeated and desperate enemy (see 12:3–9).
   A. The dragon is red (representing bloodshed), has seven heads (authority only by the will of God), and has ten horns (strength) (see 12:3).
   B. The enmity between the dragon and the woman (see 12:9) reminds us of God's edict in Genesis 3:15 after the temptation of Adam and Eve.
   C. John describes the dragon being thrown down from heaven six times (see 12:9–13) and uses the verb *ebleth*, which means "bounced."

III. The beast of the sea (see 13:1–10) embodies the four beasts Daniel described (see Daniel 7), representing world-ruling nations—likely Babylon, Persia, Media, and Greece.
   A. This sea beast represents the state—human kingdoms that reject God (see 13:4).
   B. When a nation sets out to be its own master, it turns bestial and open to demonic forces.
   C. This beast is overcome but emerges in another form intent on destroying God's children.

IV. The beast of the earth (see 13:11–18) emerges to force people to worship the first beast.
   A. This beast represents the false prophet referenced in Revelation 16, 19, and 20. He makes life dangerous and commerce difficult for those who refuse to take his mark, 666.
   B. This beast advocates putting our trust in human institutions and encourages us to compromise with worldly culture.
   C. We do not fight this beast by studying it but by knowing Jesus.

V. Confronted with this cosmic war, God's people respond with patient endurance (see 13:10).
   A. The best either beast can do is mimic God's supreme power as Creator.
   B. Our character and actions reflect who we worship. The mark of the beast represents living by human ideology.
   C. Political ideologies, whether conservative or liberal, will always be incomplete. Only the Lamb is worthy of our allegiance.

NOTES

DISCUSS | 35 MINUTES

Now discuss what you just watched by answering the following questions.

1. What is the significance of the woman in John's vision? How does the birth of her child and the appearance of the dragon represent the war between God and Satan?

2. Which of the three creatures described—the dragon, the beast out of the sea, or the beast out of the earth—stands out to you the most? What does it evoke in you?

3. Do you agree that Revelation 12–13 forms the central theological axis of Revelation? How would you summarize this big idea in a sentence or two?

4. You are living in the midst of a cosmic spiritual war zone. Given this, what priorities do you need to realign? What changes can you make to strengthen your faith?

5. John states that the relentless attacks of the enemy call for "patient endurance and faithfulness on the part of God's people" (Revelation 13:10). What does it mean for you to stand against the enemy's attacks with patience and endurance?

RESPOND | 10 MINUTES

People today have their own ideas about evil and whether or not the devil even exists. But for believers in Christ, the vision that John relates in Revelation 12–13 leaves no doubt that Satan is alive, active, and exerting all the power that he can muster on this earth. These images can feel unsettling, disturbing, and frightening. However, even as we see our enemy in focus, we must remember that Jesus has already won the battle against him! We have God's Spirit within us, empowering us as Overcomers. So take a few minutes to consider your response to this cosmic overview in Revelation 12–13. Use the questions below to help guide you in this reflection.

What image, detail, or description disturbs you the most in these chapters? Why?

How do you respond to the fact that Jesus, through His death and resurrection, has already defeated this enemy? How does this awareness change the way you view Satan and his demonic forces?

What is one way you see the spiritual battle described in these two chapters of Revelation operating in your life right now? In the world at large?

PRAY | 10 MINUTES

End your time by praying together as a group. As you pray, thank God that you have nothing to fear from the enemy because Jesus has already won the victory over the devil and his schemes. Ask God to continue to protect and guard your heart as you consider the cosmic spiritual battle going on around you. Ask if anyone has prayer requests, and then write them down so that you and your group members can continue to pray about them in the week ahead.

PERSONAL STUDY

The study for this week focuses on the enemy and his tactics. While the descriptions in Revelation 12–13 will engage your imagination, they also serve as a reminder that you are in a *spiritual battle*. Satan would like nothing more than to distract you with busyness, tempt you with comfort, and derail your faith with cultural idols. So, this week you will look at few other passages of Scripture that will reinforce your awareness of what is at stake and the importance of fulfilling your God-given purpose. As you work through these exercises, be sure to write down your responses to the questions, as you will be given a few minutes to share your insights at the start of the next session if you are doing this study with others. If you are reading *The Overcomers* alongside this study, first review chapters 7–8 in the book.

LIFE DURING WARTIME

When the United States entered World War II in December 1941, the conflict had repercussions far beyond the battlefield. Industrial and natural resources were diverted to support the war effort, which meant that sacrifices had to be made by citizens back home. Americans planted gardens (to offset the food lost by rations), went to work in factories, and prepared for possible assault by the enemy. While everyday life could appear normal at times, painful reminders of the war being waged—including the absence and loss of loved ones—was inescapable.

The cosmic war depicted in Revelation 12–13 is no different. The unholy trinity—represented by the Dragon, the beast from the sea, and the beast from the earth—continually seek "to steal and kill and destroy" the people of God (John 10:10). Jesus said of the Dragon (Satan), "He was a murderer from the beginning, not holding to the truth. . . . When he lies, he speaks his native language, for he is a liar and the father of lies" (8:44).

Jesus' statement provides a powerful summary of the message unveiled in these chapters of Revelation. The enemy is real and schemes to harm, thwart, tempt, and deceive us. But we can overcome him through the power of God's Spirit within us.

Often when we encounter life's challenges, we overlook the impact of the spiritual war that is taking place around us. We get so caught up in our pain that we fail to consider the bigger picture. We become so preoccupied with what we are experiencing that we neglect to help those around us who are in need. Instead, we tend to do what the citizens of the US did back in World War II: recognize we are in a war, realize sacrifices must be made, understand God has work for us to do in this spiritual fight, and defend against attacks from the enemy.

We cannot lose sight of the realities of life during wartime. We must rely on God's power, protecting ourselves with the spiritual armor He provides. We must arm ourselves with God's Word. We must also remain in constant communication with God by praying in the Spirit and with all kinds of prayers and requests—not only for ourselves, but also for our fellow believers who are in the war.

READ | 2 Corinthians 10:3–6; Ephesians 6:10–20; Hebrews 2:14–18

REFLECT

1. What kind of "war" are you engaged in? What weapons do you use (see 2 Corinthians 10:3–6)? What happens when you ignore that you are in such a battle?

2. What are some sacrifices you have made to avoid the temptations and snares of the devil? How have they helped you to remain focused on Christ?

> When I look at the volume of deceit, depression, fear, manipulation, death, and chaos that this mimicking unholy trinity perpetuates on my friends, family, co-workers, and the world around me, my impulse is anger and a desire to fight back. I hate the two henchmen. I want to hit back. But I know I need to take them seriously. They're extraordinarily powerful and have had thousands of years honing their craft. And yet, with the proper patience, training, and moves, we can become a real problem for these evil powers behind the world's sorrows.[34]

3. Based on Ephesians 6:10–17, what are the different pieces of armor God provides to help you defend against Satan? Why are all of these pieces of armor needed?

4. Based on Ephesians 6:17–20, how do you hit back against the enemy and force him to flee? What role does prayer play in defeating the enemy?

In the first century, our brothers and sisters would hear the Dragon being described as red not as some sort of social death or some kind of marginalization from the predominant culture but as physical death. As in being killed, murdered.... It's the endgame of the Dragon to accuse you, deceive you, and keep you asleep until he can kill you. The good news is you are an Overcomer, and that's not going to work.[35]

5. What did Jesus accomplish when He sacrificed Himself on the cross (see Hebrews 2:14–18)? How does this truth enable you to be an Overcomer who can stand against the devil?

PRAY | End your time in prayer. Ask God to strengthen, empower, and protect you against the attacks of the enemy as you accept your place in the cosmic spiritual battle.

FALSE ACCUSATIONS

One of the enemy's most potent weapons in his arsenal is *false accusations*. Satan likes to throw out lies and try to get us to believe them. As the voice that John heard in heaven said, "the accuser of our brothers and sisters . . . accuses them before our God day and night" (Revelation 12:10). Satan first accuses *us* and then accuses us *before God*.

Paul stated that "Satan himself masquerades as an angel of light" (2 Corinthians 11:14). He uses fine words and subtle deceptions to try and convince us of his skewed perspective. He does this so we will take our focus off God's truth and what *He* says about us. Satan, the great Dragon, urges us to give in to temptation by making us feel entitled, deprived, and/or deserving of more. Once we stumble and give in, he mocks us as a failure and shames us as someone unworthy of God's love—let alone anyone else's. Aiming a steady fire of accusations, the enemy's strategy is simple: to keep us away from the presence and power of Jesus.

Satan's goal is to cut us off from the power we receive in Christ to wage war against him and walk in the victory that Jesus secured over him. If the enemy can hassle us to the point where we believe God cannot love us because of our sin, then he has gained significant ground. If he can cause us to refuse to forgive others for the ways they have hurt us and disappointed us, then he has made great inroads into our hearts. If he can get us to doubt God's love and delight in us, then he has succeeded in making us feel less than we truly are. Just like Adam and Eve back in the garden of Eden, we will hide from God rather than abide in His presence.

This is why it is so important for us to pray and be familiar with the Word of God. When Jesus was being tempted in the wilderness, He used God's Word to fight back against the attacks of the enemy. He also often "withdrew to lonely places" to pray (Luke 5:16). If we likewise want to overcome our enemy, we must know God's truth so that we can see through Satan's lies—and not fail to connect frequently with our heavenly Father in prayer.

READ | Zechariah 3:1-2; Matthew 13:18-23; Matthew 4:1-11

REFLECT

1. What does the prophet Zechariah say that Satan is doing in Zechariah 3:1–2? How does this support what the heavenly voice says about the devil in Revelation 12:10?

> Despite the fact that most of the heroes of the Bible couldn't pass a background check, we often believe that we have outsinned the grace of God. Where do we get that? The Bible says, "Where sin increased, grace increased all the more" (Romans 5:20). So it's not from what the Bible teaches. It's the Dragon, the Accuser, Satan, trying to keep us asleep.[36]

2. In Jesus' parable of the sower, He describes what happens when the "seed" of God's Word falls on different kinds of hearts. What happens to the seed that falls on hearts represented by the path, rocky ground, and among thorns (see Matthew 13:18–22)? What happens to the seed that falls on the heart that represents good soil (see verse 23)?

3. What accusations does the enemy make against you most frequently? What messages come to mind when you fail, yield to temptation, or make a mistake?

4. How did Jesus fight back against Satan's temptations and accusations in Matthew 4:1–11? What does this reveal about the power of God's Word in your life?

> Life is hard. We need each other to overcome consistently. We need a safe place that holds us accountable, helps us see clearly when things are foggy, provides direction for our lives when we feel lost in it all, and expects the greatness God has placed in us to shine.[37]

5. Why is community with other believers essential to living as Overcomers? Who has helped you recently identify the enemy's lies and accusations in your life?

PRAY | End your time in prayer. Thank God for the truth of His Word that helps you see through the false accusations of the enemy. Ask the Lord today to give you clarity, wisdom, and discernment through the power of the Holy Spirit.

PURSUIT OF HOLINESS

Overcomers pursue *holiness*. In biblical terms, holiness is defined as being "separate" or "set apart."[38] Overcomers seek to be set apart from the world by not engaging in sin and by instead living in God's righteousness. Overcomers know that sin will entangle them and hinder their progress—and that no battle can be fought in such a state. So, they throw off such hinderances and fix their eyes on Jesus (see Hebrews 12:1–2).

Unfortunately, in our quest for holiness, the enemy often finds what Paul described as "a foothold" in our lives to trip us up (see Ephesians 4:27). Satan uses something we've done in the past to attack us. He employs deception, accusation, self-condemnation, and shame to limit our power in Christ and rob us of joy and peace. This typically leads to isolation. We fall into the trap of thinking no one—not even God—could love us because of our worst moments.

"Secret sins" take many different forms. Perhaps it was an affair a decade ago. Maybe it was an act of theft at the office. It could likely be an addiction. Whatever it is, we've chosen to hide our sin and never let anyone know about it—we are taking it to the grave. We have convinced ourselves that our entire world would burn to the ground if we were to confess it. We feel the weight of it daily as it crushes our peace and weakens our faith.

Secret sin locks us out of the fight. It distracts us from the spiritual realities of God's truth. Confession and repentance, on the other hand, keep us armed and dangerous against the enemy. They enable us to focus on what is true—that our lives are in God's hands and we are *new creations* in Christ (see 2 Corinthians 5:17). As Paul concluded, "Therefore, there is now no condemnation for those who are in Christ Jesus" (Romans 8:1).

Do you want to fight the enemy and secure the victory? Then drag whatever you are hiding out into the light. Confess it out loud to God, and then find a group of other Overcomers and confess it to them. Receive the grace and mercy God has already extended to you. Stand in the strength of Christ. When you pursue holiness, you land a major punch against the enemy!

READ | Ephesians 4:22–28; James 5:13–16; Psalm 51:1–19

REFLECT

1. What are some ways you currently pursue holiness in your life? How can you up your game in pursuing holiness so you can overcome the enemy's schemes against you?

2. What does Paul say in Ephesians 4:22–25 about pursuing holiness? What does it mean to not give the devil a foothold in your life (see verses 26–28)?

Darkness loses power in the light. It doesn't mean the journey is easy. When we sin, there can be significant collateral damage. But it does mean we can get untangled and out from under the soul-crushing weight of sin. There are no small sins, just sins waiting to destroy everything you're serious about loving.[39]

3. What steps does James advise you take to bring any hidden sins into the light (see James 5:13–16)? What steps do you need to take to make this happen?

4. How did David approach confession in Psalm 51:1–19? What parts of this psalm could you use as an example when it comes to confessing your own sins to God?

You need a little platoon. You need to invite people in. Encourage godly friends to help you. You need people to watch your life. You have blind spots. You have to invite them in for this purpose: to watch and encourage and engage you when you start to drift. You need to invite them in because, generally speaking, people are scared of conflict or love conflict, and both are bad. You're not asking somebody to be nitpicky about your life. You're asking for spiritual encouragement and protection.[40]

5. Who are your fellow brothers and sisters in Christ who could serve in your platoon? In what ways could those individuals provide you with spiritual encouragement and protection?

PRAY | End your time in prayer. Ask God to make you aware of any areas in your life that you have been keeping in the dark. Ask for Him to bring those sins into His light. Read through Psalm 51:1–19 again and make it your personal prayer of confession and repentance.

CONNECT & DISCUSS

Take time today to connect with a group member and talk about some of the insights from this session. Use any of the prompts below to help guide your discussion.

What is one new thing you learned or see differently now about the enemy?

How do the descriptions in Revelation 12–13 help put Satan into clearer focus?

What accusations from the enemy did you identify with God's truth this week?

Who has helped you see and experience your true identity in Christ recently? How did that person help you see the truth?

How can you help one another in your respective pursuits of holiness?

CATCH UP & READ AHEAD

Use this time to go back and complete any of the study and reflection questions from previous days that you weren't able to finish. Make a note below of any questions you've had and reflect on any growth or personal insights you've gained.

Read Revelation 14–16 and review chapter 9 in *The Overcomers* before the next group session. Use the space below to make note of anything that stands out to you or encourages you.

WEEK 6

BEFORE GROUP MEETING	Read Revelation 14–16 Review chapter 9 in *The Overcomers* Read the Welcome section (page 102)
GROUP MEETING	Discuss the Connect questions Watch the video teaching for session 6 Discuss the questions that follow as a group Do the closing exercise and pray (pages 102–106)
STUDY 1	Complete the personal study (pages 109–111)
STUDY 2	Complete the personal study (pages 112–114)
STUDY 3	Complete the personal study (pages 115–117)
CONNECT & DISCUSS	Connect with someone in your group (page 118)
CATCH UP AND READ AHEAD (BEFORE WEEK 7 GROUP MEETING)	Read Revelation 17–18 Review chapter 10 in *The Overcomers* Complete any unfinished personal studies (page 119)

YOUR FAMILY IN FAITH

"Fear God and give him glory, because the hour of his judgment has come: Worship him who made the heavens, the earth, the sea and the springs of water."

REVELATION 14:7

WELCOME | READ ON YOUR OWN

Think about the last family reunion you attended. As you connected with your fellow family members, you swapped stories about distant relatives and learned more about your ancestors. In doing so, you realized you are part of a much larger network of individuals that stretches back for generations. You share a common history.

John similarly reminds believers of their spiritual family in Revelation 14–16. He has just shown us our enemy through his portrayal of the Dragon and his two beasts—the mimicking trinity. Now, John encourages us by telling us of our family of faith. In fact, Revelation 14 features a scene of faithful believers similar to what we saw in Revelation 7:4, where we learn about our faithful predecessors. After the focus on the Dragon and the beasts, we need this touchstone with our spiritual ancestors.

John's opening scene again features 144,000 faithful followers of Jesus (a number representing completeness) who are united before God's throne. They are singing a "new song" and have remained pure in their loyalty to Jesus. The reference to virgins here echoes other biblical passages (see 2 Kings 19:21; Isaiah 37:22; 2 Corinthians 11:2) and symbolizes those who refuse to commit spiritual adultery.

You are counted among this throng of souls! So don't be discouraged by this present moment. You are part of an eternal family so big that "no one could count" its members (Revelation 7:9). Yes, the road is narrow that leads to salvation, but billions and billions of people have walked that narrow path before you. And now you follow in their spiritual footsteps as part of the same family of faith.

CONNECT | 15 MINUTES

Get the session started by choosing one or both of the following questions to discuss together as a group:

- What is something that stands out to you from last week's personal study that you would like to share with the group?

— *or* —

- Who is your most famous ancestor? How did you learn about that person?

WATCH | 20 MINUTES

Read Revelation 14–16 before you watch the video teaching. Below is an outline of the key points. Note any questions or key concepts that stand out to you.

OUTLINE

I. In Revelation 14–16, we see three angels, two harvests, and seven bowls of wrath.
   A. The first angel proclaims the gospel "to every nation, tribe, language and people" (14:6).
   B. The second angel announces Babylon has fallen (see 14:8). Babylon is code for Rome, or any empire that comes outside of God's authority.
   C. The third angel states the consequences for those who worship the Dragon (see 14:9–11).

II. Next, we see two great harvests, representing fields ripening as people turn to the Lord.
   A. The first harvest represents those people whom Jesus calls to Himself through the church by the Holy Spirit (see 14:14–16).
   B. The second harvest uses symbols to depict how Christ's atoning death on the cross covers all who repent (see 14:17–20).
   C. Both harvests show how God remains patient, "not wanting anyone to perish, but everyone to come to repentance" (2 Peter 3:9).

III. Revelation 15 shifts back to God's just wrath, contained in seven golden bowls (see 15:7).
   A. Returning to God's wrath in the seven bowls employs the literary device *recapitulation*, revealing the same story from different viewpoints.
   B. The seven bowls line up with the seven trumpets almost identically, reinforcing the heartbreaking consequences suffered by those who reject God.
   C. The seven bowls reveal the perspective of the temple from the throne of God.

IV. Revelation 16 reminds us that God's wrath is aimed at the Dragon and the beasts.
   A. God's wrath, unlike human wrath, emerges from His perfect holiness and moral law.
   B. The seven bowls reveal God giving humanity what they want—allowing them to experience the death and destruction that follow.
   C. While God's invitation to repent persists, people suffer the consequences of sin and blame God, compounding their wickedness.

V. The wrath of God will eventually be finished (see 15:1; 16:17).
   A. Unlike God's love—which is who He is and eternal—God's wrath is for a time and is finite.
   B. After the seventh bowl is emptied, a voice says, "It is done!" (16:17), echoing Jesus' words on the cross (see John 19:28–30).
   C. Revelation 14–16 reminds us that the gospel is an unstoppable force that we can share to save those who are ripe for harvest.

NOTES

DISCUSS | 35 MINUTES

Now discuss what you just watched by answering the following questions.

1. John presents us with a picture of God's faithful followers worshiping before His throne before giving us another depiction of God's wrath. Why would this have been important for John's readers? How does this scene before God's throne shape our view of what follows?

2. Ask someone in the group to read 1 John 3:16–24. According to this passage, what are some of the common family traits that followers of Jesus share? How do we recognize that we are in the same family of faith?

3. The first two angels that John sees in Revelation 14:6–8 announce the message of the gospel to the world and proclaim the fall of "Babylon the Great." How does this encourage you to remain faithful and patient as you share the good news with those around you?

4. Ask someone to read Luke 10:1–2. In light of Jesus' statement, what stands out to you about John's description of the two harvests in Revelation 14:14–20? Why?

5. Jesus said of His followers that they "are not of the world" (John 17:16). In other words, their loyalties are to God and not to Satan, "the god of this age" (2 Corinthians 4:4). What does John reveal in Revelation 16 happens to those who fail to make this distinction? How do the bowl judgments represent God giving people exactly what they want?

RESPOND | 10 MINUTES

Evangelism is a topic that evokes guilt in many believers. We all know we *should* be doing more to share the gospel with those who do not know Christ. However, rather than feeling guilty—as if sharing the gospel is a tedious obligation—we discover a more urgent motive in Revelation 14–16. We are to save those who are ripe for harvest from God's wrath! Take a few minutes on your own to think about how you communicate the gospel on a daily basis through your words, attitudes, and actions. Use the questions below to help guide you in this reflection.

Who was the person (or persons) who shared the gospel with you and/or led you to the Lord? How did they convey a sense of God's love and grace by the way they related to you?

What are some ways that you connect with unbelievers before directly sharing the gospel with them? Why is relationship so important when it comes to sharing the message of Christ?

Is there any person on your heart who does not know Christ? In addition to praying for that person, what can you do to show him or her the love and grace of Jesus?

PRAY | 10 MINUTES

End your time by praying together as a group. As you pray, ask God to give you an urgent sense of compassion for the lost as well as persistence in your relationships with those who do not know Him. Ask if anyone has prayer requests, and then write down those requests so that you and your fellow group members can continue to pray about them in the coming weeks.

PERSONAL STUDY

In this week's group time, you explored John's vision of the Lamb and the 144,000 saints. This vision reveals the importance of staying in touch with your spiritual roots and experiencing connection with other believers so that together you can endure tumultuous times. Remaining anchored within your church community is also vital for sharing the gospel with those who do not yet know Jesus as their Savior. This week, you will have the opportunity to look at a few verses to see what the Bible says about why your family of faith is so important. As you work through the exercises, be sure to continue to write down your responses to the questions. If you are reading *The Overcomers* alongside this study, first review chapter 9 in the book.

NO NEUTRALITY

The North American Treaty Organization (NATO) is a military alliance comprised of a number of countries that commit to defend each other against attacks by third parties. NATO was established on April 4, 1949, in the aftermath of World War II, and most of the countries in the organization are from Europe. But there are a handful of nations—including Switzerland, Austria, and Ireland—that have not joined NATO because they prefer to remain neutral in the world's conflicts. These nations generally do not consider themselves great powers on the world stage, and so they choose to sit out the many wars other nations get pulled into.

The same is often true when it comes to Christians participating in God's mission to seek and save the lost. Today, many believers in Christ prefer to stay "neutral" when it comes to this assignment. They believe in God and want to be moral people, but they are not comfortable in sharing certain truths in the Bible that could be perceived as controversial to others. They prefer instead to let others live the way they please as long as it isn't hurting anyone else.

God's Word, including the book of Revelation, makes it clear that this is not an option for us. Jesus taught that the "gospel of the kingdom will be preached in the whole world as a testimony to all nations, and then the end will come" (Matthew 24:14). The work of heralding the gospel is where we join in God's "alliance" to seek and save the lost from all over the world. We see this in Revelation 14:6, where the angel is proclaiming the gospel to "those who live on the earth—every nation, tribe, language and people."

You are studying Revelation right now because someone before you joined with this angel and told you, with some variation of language, to "fear God and give him glory" (verse 7). You were told that God is the Creator of all things and you should repent and worship Him. The Holy Spirit opened your eyes to believe, and you joined the 144,000 marked by Jesus and sealed with the Spirit. Now is your moment to join with God in drawing men and women unto Himself.

Don't buy the lie that you can be neutral about this!

READ | Joshua 24:14–15; Matthew 24:3–14; Luke 21:13–15

REFLECT

1. What did Joshua say to the Israelites as they prepared to enter the promised land (see Joshua 24:14–15)? What could they not remain neutral about?

2. When have you been tempted to be neutral about what other people believe and how they live their lives? Why is this not an option in light of what Jesus says in Matthew 24:4-14?

This is a type of spiritual neutrality that doesn't exist. To be indifferent to the lostness of humankind and the good news that there's a way to be reconciled with one's Creator is the way of the Dragon. There are only two sides, and everyone is on one. Unlike Switzerland, you are a major player in this great conflict. Remember that you've been uniquely wired and placed so people might seek Him and find Him.[41]

3. Do you agree that it is more loving to risk offending someone than to allow that person to eternally experience the consequences of God's wrath? Who is someone whom you need to risk offending with the message of the gospel?

4. Based on your experience and observations, how do most adult nonbelievers come to know the Lord? With this in mind, how do you go about trying to share the gospel with them?

When we're bold enough to open our lives and mouths and share the good news of the gospel with friends, family members, and neighbors, we have angelic, supernatural help. This is important because many of us shy away from sharing because we feel we don't know enough, or might get asked a question we can't answer, or aren't quick enough on our feet to have those spiritual-level conversations. The good news is, we aren't alone in it. The Spirit inside you will remind you of things you've learned or heard.[42]

5. What promises are you given in Luke 21:13–15 when it comes to sharing the gospel with other people? How does knowing that you have supernatural assistance motivate you to want to evangelize more?

PRAY | End your time in prayer. Ask God to remind you that neutrality is not an option. Invite the Holy Spirit to open your eyes to opportunities for sharing the gospel with His assistance.

HOLY HOSPITALITY

In biblical times, travelers were extremely vulnerable. The climate in most regions of the Middle East was harsh, so having access to food and water was a matter of life and death. For this reason, certain customs arose to protect travelers. A host was obligated to provide food, water, and shelter to any traveler who appeared at the door of his tent.[43]

Overcomers likewise practice hospitality as a means of protecting the people in their world who are vulnerable. They refuse to cater to any false notions in society that people should just be left to wander and fend for themselves. Instead, Overcomers meet the traveler at the door of the tent and invite him or her inside for a meal.

This kind of "holy hospitality" gives unbelievers a glimpse of God's love and opens the door for sharing the gospel with them. When we show kindness without any agenda or personal gain, people sit up and take notice. When we take time to see someone else's struggle and come alongside them, they remember. When we share the blessings we have been entrusted to steward, they experience the love of Jesus.

Holy hospitality is not merely placing flowers on the table, using the nice china, or baking homemade bread. It requires more than just having friends over for fellowship and entertainment—which often has more to do with the host than the guest. Rather, the concept of biblical hospitality has to do with welcoming in the stranger—or maybe even the enemy.

Many of us have been immersed in "stranger danger" our whole lives. We've been so conditioned to defend against the harm that others could cause us that we pass by those in need and assume someone else will help. But biblical hospitality goes the extra mile for people. It washes dirty feet and stops to help those who have been left on the roadside.

The Bible reveals that when we practice the compassion of Jesus and show holy hospitality in this way, we are doing it for the Lord. As Jesus said, "Truly I tell you, whatever you did for one of the least of these brothers and sisters of mine, you did for me" (Matthew 25:40). Protect the vulnerable!

READ | 1 Peter 4:7–11; Luke 10:25–37; Matthew 5:43–47

REFLECT

1. When have you recently practiced biblical hospitality in the manner described in 1 Peter 4:7–11? What motivated your gift of hospitality in that situation?

How do we make war against the beasts? Not with their weapons. Not with violence. Not with shaming. Not with mocking. Not with belittling. That isn't how we make war. To do so would be to join the beasts in what they're doing and become like them. . . . To fight is to confess, to repent, to fill our lives with worship and prayer, and it looks like hospitality. It looks like dining room tables with people who are different from us sitting around them so that we might show them the love of God that we've received as His people. These things must be woven into the makeup of our lives.[44]

2. Check any of the descriptions of hospitality below that reflect something you've done in the past six months:

- ☐ Stopped to talk and listen to someone from another culture or belief system.
- ☐ Invited new neighbors to your home for a meal or dessert.
- ☐ Provided food, clothing, medicine, or school supplies to someone in need.
- ☐ Volunteered to serve a single parent, homeless person, widow, or orphan.
- ☐ Visited an incarcerated inmate and/or corresponded with them.
- ☐ Changed your plans in order to help someone injured or in crisis.

3. Does this kind of holy hospitality come naturally to you, or do you have to be intentional about it? In either case, how do you practice it consistently as part of your everyday life?

4. What stands out to you in reading the parable of the good Samaritan in Luke 10:25–37? How does Jesus illustrate hospitality in this parable?

Overcomers practice radically ordinary hospitality as a weapon against evil and despair in this present darkness. Compromise happens when we cater to the predominant culture's values that stand opposed to the reign and rule of Jesus. Compromise also happens when we choose our own comfort and control over the mission of God to love and serve those who are far from God. . . . Hospitality looks like this: "Love your enemies and pray for those who persecute you" (Matthew 5:44).[45]

5. What is Jesus' point about holy hospitality in Matthew 5:43–47? Why does following His command require you to go beyond merely loving those you already love?

PRAY | End your time in prayer. Ask God to give you the courage, creativity, and compassion to show radical holy hospitality to someone in need of help this coming week.

BABYLON HAS FALLEN

As previously noted, John sees an angel in Revelation 14:6 who proclaims the gospel of Jesus "to those who live on the earth." The angel instructs the inhabitants of the world to fear God, give Him glory, and honor Him in worship as their Creator. This is followed by a second angel who makes a proclamation of the gospel from a different angle. The second angel says, "Fallen! Fallen is Babylon the Great" (verse 8).

Babylon was an ancient city located on the Euphrates River in what is today the nation of Iraq. It was the cultural and political center of the Babylonian Empire, which under King Nebuchadnezzar laid siege to Jerusalem in 597 BC, destroying the temple and carrying many of its inhabitants into exile. In John's day, Babylon was code for Rome. It represented all the wickedness and idolatry of the world system that stood in opposition to God.

So, the angel here is not speaking of a literal Babylon but is referencing the conflict between *spiritual* Babylon and the church. The angel is proclaiming that the system in which the people of the world are placing their trust is bankrupt and broken. As we read in 1 John 2:16-17, "Everything in the world—the lust of the flesh, the lust of the eyes, and the pride of life—comes not from the Father but from the world. The world and its desires pass away, but whoever does the will of God lives forever."

The angel's proclamation resonates as much today as it did when John first wrote the book of Revelation. This world is broken. It offers no hope of salvation. And those who put their trust in it will only find that it is fallen and has failed them. As Overcomers, we have the opportunity to join with the second angel and let people know there is another way. We can point them to the God who offers them wholeness, hope, and salvation. We can proclaim the good news to those who need to be shaken out of their spiritual slumber.

In John 6:68, Peter said to Jesus, "You have the words of eternal life." *You* have words of eternal life that the lost in this world need to hear. *You* are the friend that they need. *You* are in proximity. *You* have the gift of supernatural help to offer to them.

READ | 2 Corinthians 4:1-6; Acts 17:24-34; Luke 15:11-24

REFLECT

1. What does Paul say in 2 Corinthians 4:1–4 about the god of this age? What must Overcomers do to help the spiritually blind restore their sight (see verses 5–6)?

2. How does Paul's message on Mars Hill (see Acts 17:24–34) illustrate a "Babylon has fallen" moment? How does Paul tailor the gospel message to his audience?

Luke 15 holds one of the more beautiful sentences in the Bible. Speaking of the prodigal son who had destroyed his life pursuing Babylon, we read, *"But when he came to his senses."* When he woke up, he was determined to rise and go to his father. Here's where we come in as men and women wake up to the reality that Babylon has fallen. As Overcomers, we proclaim the good news to those who are shaken out of their slumber by the brokenness of this world.[46]

3. In the parable of the prodigal son (see Luke 15:11-24), how did "coming to his senses" motivate the younger son to return home to his father, in spite of his offense? How did his father's response exceed the son's expectations?

4. When have you recently been there for someone who "came to their senses" and realized they were living in the rubble of a fallen Babylon? How did you minister to that person?

Humankind is meant to dwell in the presence of God. Where that is, the predominant posture of humanity flourishes; but the further we move from this, the more sexually perverse and violent we become. The brokenness and perversion of our day is leading people to ask deeper and more spiritual questions. As Overcomers, we need to be prepared to give them a real answer.[47]

5. Do you agree that the brokenness and perversion of our day is prompting more people to ask spiritual questions? When have you recently encountered a situation reflecting this?

PRAY | End your time in prayer. Ask God to guide you to individuals whose Babylon has fallen, leaving them open to considering the message of the gospel. Pray for ways to engage and challenge them with the power of God's love through Jesus Christ.

CONNECT & DISCUSS

Take time today to connect with a group member and talk about some of the insights from this session. Use any of the prompts below to help guide your discussion.

What is one new thing you learned this week about the importance of sharing the gospel with those who need Christ?

How did your understanding of holy hospitality change or expand this week?

How can you use your own painful seasons to meet others after their "Babylon" has fallen?

What image, detail, or description especially stands out to you from Revelation 14–16? Why do you think it resonates so strongly with you right now?

What is one change you will make this week because of what you're learning in this study?

CATCH UP & READ AHEAD

Use this time to go back and complete any of the study and reflection questions from previous days that you weren't able to finish. Make a note below of any questions you've had and reflect on any growth or personal insights you've gained.

Read Revelation 17–18 and review chapter 10 in *The Overcomers* before the next group session. Use the space below to make note of anything that stands out to you or encourages you.

WEEK 7

BEFORE GROUP MEETING	Read Revelation 17–18 Review chapter 10 in *The Overcomers* Read the Welcome section (page 122)
GROUP MEETING	Discuss the Connect questions Watch the video teaching for session 7 Discuss the questions that follow as a group Do the closing exercise and pray (pages 122–126)
STUDY 1	Complete the personal study (pages 129–131)
STUDY 2	Complete the personal study (pages 132–134)
STUDY 3	Complete the personal study (pages 135–137)
CONNECT & DISCUSS	Connect with someone in your group (page 138)
CATCH UP AND READ AHEAD (BEFORE WEEK 8 GROUP MEETING)	Read Revelation 19–22 Review chapters 11–12 in *The Overcomers* Complete any unfinished personal studies (page 139)

YOUR CULTURAL CAUTION

"Hallelujah! Salvation and glory and power belong to our God, for true and just are his judgments. He has condemned the great prostitute who corrupted the earth by her adulteries. He has avenged on her the blood of his servants."

REVELATION 19:1–2

WELCOME | READ ON YOUR OWN

Long before Charles Dickens contrasted the cities of London and Paris in *A Tale of Two Cities*, the book of Revelation revealed a more sobering contrast of two cities: Babylon and the New Jerusalem. Each city in John's vision represents specific cultural values and carries its own set of artifacts, attitudes, and actions.

After the wrath of God has been expended with the seven golden bowls, we are shown one of the most unsettling scenes in the entire Bible—a prostitute riding on the beast out of the sea. The intention of Jesus, the originator of John's message, seems clear: to present both the first-century church and the church of today with a caution about losing our focus and shifting our loyalties.

Throughout the Bible, we see people building cities and creating idols in rebellion against God. We see it in Genesis when the people build the Tower of Babel. We see it with Pharaoh in Egypt, who enslaved God's people to build an empire. We see it with Nebuchadnezzar and the literal Babylon. Throughout history, people built cities, institutions, and edifices as the basis for their purpose and power.

In Revelation 17–19, we get a glimpse of what life looks like when we build a civilization unto ourselves and settle for earthly pleasures and power. We see that we can either align with the prostitute and the beast in creating our own Babylon, or we can accept Jesus' invitation to experience His finished work in the New Jerusalem where all things have been made new.

CONNECT | 15 MINUTES

Get the session started by choosing one or both of the following questions to discuss together as a group:

- What is something that spoke to your heart in last week's personal study that you would like to share with the group?

— *or* —

- What are the most dangerous cultural temptations faced by believers today? Why do you believe these are especially dangerous?

WATCH | 20 MINUTES

Read Revelation 17–18 before you watch the video teaching. Below is an outline of the key points. Note any questions or key concepts that stand out to you.

OUTLINE

I. Revelation 17–18 warns that we must stay the course if we want to reach the New Jerusalem.
   A. The prostitute riding the first beast (see Revelation 13) expresses both the lewd immorality and seductive charm found in Babylon.
   B. Understanding the symbolism of this scene requires "a mind with wisdom" (17:9)—the original recipients assumed Babylon represented Rome.
   C. The kings of the earth are drawn to the prostitute. Even John was "greatly astonished" when he saw her (17:6).

II. Babylon and the cities of man that it symbolizes are always built on unreliable foundations.
   A. They are built on folly, pleasure, comfort, and earthly security.
   B. They are built on the temporal—what they offer can be stolen or destroyed, or it can deteriorate.
   C. They are built on illusions, appearing to offer one thing but providing another, just the opposite of the Beatitudes (see Matthew 5:3–12).

III. Babylon always ends up consuming and destroying herself (see Revelation 17:16).
   A. Her insatiable consumption ultimately devours itself—nothing can satisfy her appetite for more.
   B. Consequently, she becomes a dwelling place for demons (see 18:2).
   C. In decay and ruin, she is haunted by the unclean and filled with filth.

IV. Her demise exposes all of her weak foundations and false illusions.
   A. She loses all blessing and attributes and is reduced to nothing.
   B. Her ruin fulfills the prediction of judgment (see 18:6–8), similar to Sodom and Egypt.
   C. Her beneficiaries mourn because they lose their riches and privileges (see 18:19–20).

V. God's people are called to practice living in holiness, an all-new plausibility structure (see 18:4–5).
   A. Holy living is characterized by peace (rejecting the violence of Babylon) and generosity (rejecting the consumption of Babylon).
   B. Holy living is also known by its purity (rejecting the sexual immorality of Babylon) and radical hospitality (rejecting the prejudice of Babylon).
   C. This call warns God's people to avoid the seductive spell of Babylon and not live under her influence.

NOTES

DISCUSS | 35 MINUTES

Now discuss what you just watched by answering the following questions.

1. What stands out to you in the description of the great prostitute in Revelation 17:3–6? What is significant about her attire, her adornments, and what she is "drunk" on?

2. John was "greatly astonished" when he saw the prostitute (verse 6). What do you think so captivated John about her? What does this say about the seduction of what she represents?

3. What does the angel inform John will ultimately happen to the prostitute (see verses 15–18)? What does this say about the way that Satan operates in this world?

4. How do the kings, merchants, and captains of the earth respond when they hear of Babylon's fall? What does this say about the hearts of people in the world today?

5. Ask someone to read Romans 12:2. How does this passage echo the call to live apart from the world? What does it mean for you to not conform to the pattern of this world?

RESPOND | 10 MINUTES

Babylon has a subtle way of attracting our attention that can be difficult for us to pinpoint. As eternal beings living in mortal bodies, we have to function within certain civic, social, and cultural structures. Yet even as we go to work, participate in our community, and enjoy our family and friends, we are called to holy living. Dwelling in Babylon causes us to miss out on the peace, joy, and fellowship with other believers that God wants us to have in our lives.

What is your biggest takeaway from Revelation 17–19? How is that relevant in your life right now?

When have you had to set a boundary or step away from a "Babylon"? What was appealing about it?

Of the four characteristics of holy living mentioned—peace, generosity, purity, and hospitality—which one is most prevalent in your life? Which one could use a little more practice and cultivation?

PRAY | 10 MINUTES

End your time by praying together. Thank God for allowing you to see the truth about human creations and Babylonian idols. Ask Him to protect your heart as you serve as His ambassador in this world. Ask if anyone has prayer requests, and then write down those requests so that you and other group members can continue to pray about them in the week ahead.

PERSONAL STUDY

As you learned in this week's group time, the "Babylons" of this world continually try to pull you away from your first love: Christ. Babylon promises a better, more comfortable, and more manageable life—but the subtle compromises it requires will lead you away from God's way. Babylon serves as a reminder that in God's kingdom, the first shall be last and the last shall be first. This week, you have the opportunity to focus on the Beatitudes and the values of the New Jerusalem—peace, generosity, purity, and hospitality. As you work through the exercises, be sure to write down your responses to the questions, as you will be given an opportunity to share your insights at the start of the next session if you are doing this study with others. If you are reading *The Overcomers* alongside this study, first review chapter 10 in the book.

JUST ONE LOOK

In Greek mythology, Aphrodite was considered to be the most beautiful of the goddesses. Yet she also brought about great chaos. Aphrodite was married to Hephaestus, the god of fire and metalworking, but she was not faithful to him. In fact, Greek mythology states she seduced a number of other gods, including Hermes, Poseidon, and Ares. When Hephaestus learned of her unfaithfulness, he tried to exact revenge, but his plot backfired and caused him more shame.[48]

In Revelation 17, we encounter a similar figure who has great powers of seduction. As John wrote, "The woman was dressed in purple and scarlet, and was glittering with gold, precious stones and pearls. She held a golden cup in her hand, filled with abominable things and the filth of her adulteries" (verse 4). This seductress hides behind luxury and opulence. She rides the beast of the sea (see 13:1), compelling the people of Earth to shift their affection and worship from Jesus to governmental structures and systems.

The woman commands attention. Even John admitted, "When I saw her, I was greatly astonished" (17:6). John, one of the original twelve disciples, was so sucked in by her beauty that he had to be rebuked by the angel (see verse 7). If the apostle whom Jesus loved, who rested his head on the Savior's chest at the Last Supper (see John 13:23), can look at her and marvel, it means that all followers of Jesus are vulnerable as well. She is a seductress . . . and she's better at it than most of us think.

John stated that the name written on the woman's forehead is a mystery: "BABYLON THE GREAT, THE MOTHER OF PROSTITUTES, AND OF THE ABOMINATIONS OF THE EARTH" (Revelation 17:5). She is drunk on the blood of God's people (see verse 6). Later, the angel revealed, "The woman you saw is the great city that rules over the kings of the earth" (verse 18). She represents what humankind can build in rebellion to God. The picture is of a city that exalts itself as divine over God.

The woman is seductive, and she is dangerous. So John warns us to watch out for her. She entices and promises comfort, freedom, and meaning. But in the end, like all the enemy's schemes, her seductions lead to shame, bondage, chaos, and destruction.

READ | Romans 12:1–2; John 4:10–14; 1 Corinthians 10:11–13

REFLECT

1. What attributes of culture do you find attractive and appealing? Are you drawn more to beauty, youth, and sex appeal, or power, wealth, and security? Explain.

2. What does it mean to conform to the pattern of the world (see Romans 12:1-2)? What are some ways you can safeguard yourself from the seductive allure of today's culture?

This is what the prostitute does. This is her song. "Life is found in me. Submit. Surrender. This is the way you should live." It's built on an illusion. It promises comfort and ease and sensual satisfaction, but the reality is she cannot deliver on those promises. She has no power by which to fulfill those promises.[49]

3. When have you been disappointed by something you pursued that promised more than it could deliver? What cultural illusions tend to tempt you the most?

4. What does Jesus say in John 4:10–14 about the life that He came to bring? Why is true satisfaction and purpose in life found only in Him?

The prostitute is promising . . . your best life. . . . "Yeah, life is hard. Do you know what would make it better? This kind of sexual sensuality. You should get into that. Do you know what would make it better? Great wealth, and I have great wealth. Serve me. Follow me. Bow to me. Worship me. I'll keep you safe. I'll make sure your life is good. I'll make sure you're happy. Jesus isn't going to make you happy. Why would you go to Him? Look how rigid His rules are. He's always trying to take from you, saying, 'Don't do *this* and don't do *this* and don't do *this*.'"[50]

5. What risk do you take when you assume you are immune to culture's influence? What warning does Paul provide in this regard in 1 Corinthians 10:11–13?

PRAY | End your time in prayer. Ask God to guard your heart and give you wisdom about how to live without succumbing to the seduction of cultural compromise. Listen for the Holy Spirit's instruction on areas of your life where you need to look away from cultural temptation.

A HOLY NATION

Whether you realize it or not, you are either moving toward Babylon or toward the New Jerusalem. You are either focused on the narrow path leading you toward God's holiness or you are being drawn off-road into the wilderness of the world. Babylon and the New Jerusalem represent two different kingdoms with two different cultural value systems. They are at war with one another—and you are living in one of them.

This becomes apparent when you look at the contrast between the foundational principles of each city. The New Jerusalem is built on the principles that Jesus defined in the Sermon on the Mount. In God's city, "Blessed are the poor in spirit" (Matthew 5:3); "blessed are the meek" (verse 5); "blessed are the merciful" (verse 7); "blessed are the pure in heart" (verse 8); and "blessed are the peacemakers" (verse 9).

Babylon is built on the principles that the prostitute promotes. In Satan's city, "Blessed are the wealthy"; "blessed are the powerful"; "blessed are the self-serving"; "blessed are those who do what they want"; and "blessed are those who make war." Jesus ends His principles with, "Blessed are those who are persecuted because of righteousness" (verse 10). Babylon ends with, "Blessed are you when you persecute those who force you to live by their standards."

Overcomers are to live in a way that presents a different plausibility structure to the world. Overcomers reject the violence of Babylon and choose to be peacemakers. In contrast to the insatiable consumption of Babylon, their lives reflect radical generosity. Overcomers reject Babylon's promise of soul-level satisfaction through sexual gratification and uphold God's intention for human sexuality.

Overcomers take Jesus at His word when He says, "I am the way and the truth and the life. No one comes to the Father except through me" (John 14:6). They resist the hatred, exclusivity, and divisiveness of Babylon and instead choose the way of Jesus characterized by love, inclusivity, and unity. They keep their wits about them. Revelation warns of the dangers of flirting with culture and reminds us that we are a holy nation. In sharp contrast to the seduction and destruction of Babylon, we are known by God's love and redemption.

READ | Matthew 5:1–12; Psalm 2:1–6; Acts 3:19–20

REFLECT

1. After reading the Beatitudes in Matthew 5:1–12, how would you summarize the key distinction between your life in God's kingdom and the life offered by Babylon?

2. Which of the Beatitudes resonates the most with you right now? Which one challenges you to be more intentional in how you live?

> Why does Babylon always end in violence for the people of God? They think we're trying to rob them of life. The reason the nations rage against God and His people is that the way we live is an offense to them—first, because it calls them to something different and, second, because it shows a plausibility structure where humanity flourishes without worshiping the beast or bending the knee to this prostitute.[51]

3. What does the psalmist write in Psalm 2:1–3 about the nations of the world conspiring against God? How does God respond to their efforts (see verses 4–6)?

4. How does living out our faith based on God's standards offend the power structure and lifestyle trends of those who are living in old Babylon?

> With just a glance at her, we can be sucked in. Repentance is a gift that needs to be specific and actionable, so let's be mindful of what we're repenting of and what it looks like to walk in an opposite direction. . . . Remember, the holiness of God destroys and decimates everything that isn't pure and perfect. Return to God's mercy and live by His presence and power. Turn from the lies of "Babylon the great, mother of prostitutes and of earth's abominations" back into the arms of a holy and merciful God.[52]

5. Why does repentance need to be specific and actionable in order to redirect you to God? What does Peter say in Acts 3:19–20 about the purpose of repentance?

PRAY | End your time in prayer. Ask God to help you expound the principles of God's kingdom to the world. Pray that more and more people would be brought into the New Jerusalem.

SPIRITUAL SECURITY

In Revelation 15:1, John wrote, "I saw in heaven another great and marvelous sign: seven angels with the seven last plagues—last, because with them God's wrath is completed." After witnessing the horrendous scene of the prostitute riding the beast, and before seeing what happens next on the earth, we need to be reminded that for Christians, *God's wrath is over.* As Paul wrote, "Since we have now been justified by his blood, how much more shall we be saved from God's wrath through him!" (Romans 5:9). We are now under God's mercy.

God's wrath is rooted in His holiness and the weight of His glory. He desires that all people be saved and that none perish (see 2 Peter 3:9). So it's not rage that you are witnessing in the pages of Revelation when you read about God's wrath. It's pure priestly fire. "The wrath of God is being revealed from heaven against all the godlessness and wickedness of people, who suppress the truth by their wickedness" (Romans 1:18).

So many Christians live their lives as though they are still under the wrath of God. They overlook what John wrote in his Gospel: "Whoever believes in the Son has eternal life, but whoever rejects the Son will not see life, for God's wrath remains on them" (John 3:36). God's wrath is not on those who have accepted Christ. When you wake up each day, all that is waiting for you are God's compassions—for "they are new every morning" (Lamentations 3:23).

Wouldn't it be great to just believe what the Bible actually says about your status before God? When He looks at you, He sees a beloved son or daughter. As Paul wrote, "Because you are his sons, God sent the Spirit of his Son into our heart, the Spirit who calls out, '*Abba*, Father'" (Galatians 4:6). God sees a person who has been sealed with the Holy Spirit (see Ephesians 1:13–14). He sees a treasured possession (see 1 Peter 2:9).

So refuse to let the enemy cast doubt in your mind about where you stand with God. Choose instead to see God as your loving heavenly Father. Your eternal security is in Christ.

READ | Romans 8:31–34; Hebrews 13:5–6; James 1:16–18

REFLECT

1. When have you felt like God was angry with you or directing His wrath at you? What does Paul say in Romans 8:31–34 that proves this is *not* true?

> What you see in the Bible isn't clean and stable lives but messy, complicated, broken people with God right in the middle of every day—sustaining, encouraging, and reminding them of His grace. Because you're a child of God, you're not under wrath but mercy. . . . When suffering comes, regardless of its form, you can look to your heavenly Father, who loves you and has not abandoned you.[53]

2. What promise does God make to you in Hebrews 13:5–6? What are some challenges in your life that tend to obscure the fact that God is always with you?

3. How do you consider God's wrath differently based on your study of Revelation? What stands out to you about the connection between God's wrath and His love?

> Unlike God's love, His wrath has an expiration date. The wrath of God will eventually be finished forever. Remember, God is love (see 1 John 4:8). That will never change. Sixty trillion years from now, the triune God of the Bible will be perfect in love, lavishing that love on His adopted sons and daughters who through faith and grace alone have come into His kingdom out from under wrath and into His mercy.[54]

4. What does James say about God's nature (see James 1:16–18)? How does it reassure you to know that God's love for you will never end?

5. How is an ongoing awareness of God's mercy a source of power for you? Who is a fellow brother or sister in Christ who needs to be reminded of God's mercy?

PRAY | End your time in prayer. Ask God to remind you of His mercy and kindness toward you. Allow Him to dispel any false assumptions the enemy has planted in your heart and mind that God is angry with you. Thank Him for the gift of grace through Jesus.

CONNECT & DISCUSS

Take time today to connect with a group member and talk about some of the insights from this session. Use any of the prompts below to help guide your discussion.

What is one thing that stood out this week from your personal study?

Which verse or Scripture passage that you studied spoke directly to your heart this week?

What did you see differently about the culture you live in this week?

How does this week's study challenge you to leave Babylon behind and seek the New Jerusalem?

What is one change you want to make as a result of this week's study? Why?

CATCH UP & READ AHEAD

Use this time to go back and complete any of the study and reflection questions from previous days that you weren't able to finish. Make a note below of any questions you've had and reflect on any growth or personal insights you've gained.

Read Revelation 19–22 and review chapters 11–12 in *The Overcomers* before the next group session. Use the space below to make note of anything that stands out to you or encourages you.

WEEK 8

BEFORE GROUP MEETING	Read Revelation 19–22 Review chapters 11–12 in *The Overcomers* Read the Welcome section (page 142)
GROUP MEETING	Discuss the Connect questions Watch the video teaching for session 8 Discuss the questions that follow as a group Do the closing exercise and pray (pages 142–146)
STUDY 1	Complete the personal study (pages 149–151)
STUDY 2	Complete the personal study (pages 152–154)
STUDY 3	Complete the personal study (pages 155–157)
CONNECT & DISCUSS	Connect with someone in your group (page 158)
WRAP IT UP	Complete any unfinished personal studies (page 158) Connect with your group about the next study that you want to go through together

YOUR NEW HOME

*"Hallelujah! For our Lord God Almighty reigns.
Let us rejoice and be glad and give him glory!
For the wedding of the Lamb has come, and
his bride has made herself ready. Fine linen,
bright and clean, was given her to wear."*

REVELATION 19:6-8

WELCOME | READ ON YOUR OWN

For followers of Christ, the final chapters of Revelation offer incredible encouragement. So far, we have seen many vivid images and heartbreaking symbols of God's judgment on those who reject Him. We've explored the allure of Babylon, seen her destruction, and reaffirmed our commitment to holy living. Now, we are called to celebrate Jesus' victory as it floods over the creative order and makes all things new.

It seems fitting that the wedding of the Lamb invites us to participate in a heavenly banquet celebrating the triumph of Jesus. This meal transcends birthday suppers, Christmas dinners, and earthly wedding receptions. This heavenly feast of victory is slow, intentional, deliberate, and joyful. It ushers us into experiencing our new home as heaven converges with earth. There, we enjoy the renewed earth, new physical bodies, and the end of death, disease, and mourning. Our reward is made complete and our faith becomes sight as we dwell in the full-access presence of Jesus.

Remember that the overarching purpose of the book of Revelation is to embolden believers' confidence in Jesus . . . come what may. These final chapters punctuate our confidence by revealing what awaits us: a literal place, with literal people, in the presence of the living God—the Maker of Heaven and Earth. The best is yet to come!

"This world is not our home; we are looking forward to our everlasting home in heaven. With Jesus' help we will continually offer our sacrifice of praise to God by telling others of the glory of his name" (Hebrews 13:14–15 TLB). Once there, our joy will be complete and our suffering will end. We will be in our new forever home.

CONNECT | 15 MINUTES

Get this final session started by choosing one or both of the following questions to discuss together as a group:

- What is something that stands out from last week's personal study that you would like to share with the group?

  — or —

- When was the last time you enjoyed a meal celebrating a special occasion? What made the time so special?

WATCH | 20 MINUTES

Read Revelation 19–22 before you watch the video teaching. Below is an outline of the key points. Note any questions or key concepts that stand out to you.

OUTLINE

I. Revelation 19:6–22 reveals the wedding feast of the Lamb, the millennium reign of Jesus, and our new home with Jesus.

   A. The wedding feast of the Lamb (see 19:6–8) celebrates the ultimate victory of King Jesus and His marriage with the church.

   B. Meals are significant in celebrating God's grace for His people, as seen in the Passover meal, Psalm 23, and the Lord's Supper.

   C. As Overcomers, we are invited to partake of this meal in the presence of Jesus.

II. Jesus reigns with and through His people for a millennium (see 20:6).

   A. There are three orthodox views of this reign: premillennialism, postmillennialism, and amillennialism.

   B. Jesus is described as the King of kings, a victorious and regal warrior (see 19:11–16).

   C. God's kingdom is already here (see Mark 1:14–15) and Satan is defeated (see Revelation 20:7–10).

III. Heaven comes down and is a literal place that God has renewed and remade (see 21:1–7).

   A. We often inaccurately view heaven as intangible, but the Bible is clear it is a literal place (see 2 Peter 3:8–10; Isaiah 35).

   B. God is not going to concede the earth to His enemies. Throughout Scripture, He redeems His creation for His purposes.

   C. The Christian vision for the future is that of a renewed world, not a brand-new heaven.

IV. God gathers up the full range of the world's ethnic diversity and unites us all as His people.

   A. No one ethnic group or culture can reveal the full image of God—it requires all of us.

   B. When heaven converges with earth, it will feature a physical place with peoples, kings, and cultures (see 21:24).

   C. Our future home includes not only a renewed physical earth but a renewed creativity and calling for God's people.

V. The greatest reward is that we will be in the presence of Jesus (see 21:22; 22:4).

   A. This is what we were made for, our eternal reward: to dwell in the presence of God.

   B. In God's presence, there are no tears, death, disease, mourning, or crying (see 21:4); no temple (see 21:22); and no closed gates (see 21:25).

   C. We will see God face-to-face because we have been transformed (see 22:4).

NOTES

DISCUSS | 35 MINUTES

Now discuss what you just watched by answering the following questions.

1. Ask someone to read Revelation 19:1–10. What stands out to you in this invitation to the wedding feast of the Lamb? What is the role of worship in this celebration?

2. Of the three orthodox views of the millennium—premillennialism, postmillennialism, and amillennialism—which one do you tend to hold? Why is any such view not as important as the fact that Jesus' ultimate victory is being celebrated?

3. What surprises you the most about the physical, literal reality of heaven as described in Revelation 21–22? What do you think has been the basis for your expectations about heaven?

4. After John sees the New Jerusalem descend from heaven, the One seated on the throne says, "I am making everything new!" (21:5). What call does He then make to His followers? Who does He say will inherit all these riches (see verses 6-7)?

5. John's vision ends with an invitation: "Let the one who is thirsty come; and let the one who wishes take the free gift of the water of life" (22:17). How are you accepting His invitation today? What feelings do you experience when you consider being face-to-face with Jesus?

RESPOND | 10 MINUTES

Revelation ends with quite the big reveal, and there's a lot to take in. As you consider these final scenes, pay attention to how your heart is responding to the unveiling of your new heavenly home. What evokes excitement and joy? What confuses or concerns you? Regardless of your reaction now, know that when heaven converges with earth and is remade by God, you will experience more joy, peace, fulfillment, and gratitude than you can presently imagine. You will be with your family of faith in the midst of ultimate reality in your forever home.

What images from these final scenes in Revelation stand out and linger with you?

What remains uncertain or confusing to you about heaven based on what you read? What one question would you want to ask John to help alleviate your concerns?

Consider and discuss with your group the possibility of planning a meal together as a foretaste of the Lamb's wedding feast as well as a fitting way to celebrate concluding this study. What are some of the things you would need to make this occasion extraordinary without too much effort or expense?

PRAY | 10 MINUTES

End your time by praying together as a group. Thank God for the experience of learning with your fellow brothers and sisters in Christ. Praise Jesus for the victory you all share as you anticipate your heavenly home. Follow up on previous prayer requests and ask if anyone would like any ongoing prayer as your study concludes. Write down those requests so that you and other group members can continue to pray about them moving forward.

PERSONAL STUDY

As you saw in this week's group time, the final chapters in Revelation depict the glorious celebration that will occur at Jesus' victorious arrival and the new eternal home that God has prepared for you—where you will bask in His presence. While you will continue to face challenges and suffering in this broken world, you can always cling to this confident reassurance that is offered in Revelation. No matter what world events occur or what circumstances you encounter, you know that God *is* still on His throne, that your salvation *is* secure because of what Jesus did on the cross, and that your heavenly home *does* await you. As you complete the exercises, be sure to continue to write down your responses to the questions. If you are reading *The Overcomers* alongside this study, first review chapters 11–12 in the book.

VICTORY CELEBRATION

What comes to mind when you picture a dining room table? Maybe you recall all the Thanksgivings you spent at your grandmother's house around the table. Perhaps you have memories of playing games with your nephews and nieces at the table. You might remember times that you spent sharing a meal at the table with close friends.

Whatever comes to mind, the image is likely one of *fellowship* and *friendship*. So it's no surprise that as we get to the end of Revelation, we find God gathering His people together around a shared meal. "Let us rejoice and be glad and give him glory! For the wedding of the Lamb has come, and his bride has made herself ready" (Revelation 19:7).

In Revelation 19, a chapter setting up the final battle between good and evil, the vanquishing of Satan, and the arrival of King Jesus, we have a table, a feast, and the saints of God dressed in fine linen. Looking back on the history of God's people, a table set in the presence of a soon-vanquished enemy is a familiar scene. For instance, in Psalm 23:5, King David wrote, "You prepare a table before me in the presence of my enemies."

But perhaps the most direct historical connection comes from the Passover meal established at the end of the plagues unleashed on Egypt. The Israelites had been enslaved in Egypt for generations when God chose Moses to lead them into the promised land. After the ninth plague, God commanded His people to prepare a meal. God told them to get an unblemished lamb—the best they had—and prepare unleavened bread, gather bitter herbs, and dress for action. They were to put the lamb's blood on the doorposts of their homes, signaling the angel of death to pass them by as God's wrath descended on all the firstborn sons of Egypt.

For the next 1,600 years, God's people would gather together to celebrate the Passover. As they ate the Passover meal in homes, they anchored themselves in God's story for them. Similarly, the wedding feast of the Lamb invites us to realize all we have seen, experienced, and endured as Overcomers to get to this point. God invites us to join Him and relish the feast He has prepared for us. We will celebrate the victory secured by Jesus once and for all.

READ | Psalm 105:1–7; Exodus 12:1–20; Matthew 26:26–29

REFLECT

1. The Passover, and other sacred feasts in Israel, reminded the people of God's faithfulness. What does the psalmist say we should likewise remember about God (see Psalm 105:1–7)?

> What do you think God is trying to teach His people at the table? What was He calling them into the wilderness for? Exodus says it was "to hold a feast to me." The feast that frees them from slavery is a feast over time that forms them as people of God. They come back to it over and over and over again as they gather, anchoring themselves in their story, not getting lost in the one that's projected to them all around.[55]

2. What does the wedding feast of the Lamb have in common with the Passover meal described in Exodus 12:1–20? How is it distinctly different?

3. How do the sacred meals described in these passages differ from the way we tend to regard meals today? When have you experienced a meal that felt holy in its celebration?

4. How did Jesus transform the Passover meal into what we know as the Last Supper (see Matthew 26:26–29)? What did Jesus want His disciples to remember by celebrating this meal together after His death and resurrection?

In gathering like this, our minds are reminded of God's good grace, our souls are nurtured, and our community is strengthened as we practice for the coming feast where all things will be made new.[56]

5. What traditions have you created to remember what God has done for you in the past? How have these traditions helped you to trust Him for the future?

PRAY | End your time in prayer. Thank God for His invitation to the wedding feast of the Lamb and for the ways you get a taste of this celebration in earthly gatherings.

TROPHY OF TRIUMPH

Being an Overcomer includes royal privilege and power because of our relationship with our King. When Jesus, our heavenly warrior, defeats the Dragon and his forces once and for all (see Revelation 20:10), we will celebrate and move into our new eternal home. However, we do not have to wait until this takes place to vanquish the enemy of our soul and his demons.

The kingdom of God is already underway! If we worship and follow Jesus, we will be empowered to overcome the enemy and take back what the devil has stolen. When Jesus first began His ministry, He announced to the people, "The time has come. . . . The kingdom of God has come near. Repent and believe the good news!" (Mark 1:15). The rule and reign of God was embodied in Jesus as He took on flesh and dwelt among humankind.

Jesus not only ushered in the kingdom of God but also empowered His followers. At one point in His ministry, He appointed seventy-two disciples and sent them out ahead of Him to the towns and places where He was about to go. When these disciples returned, they proclaimed, "Lord, even the demons submit to us in your name" (Luke 10:17). The seventy-two disciples received kingdom authority over the principalities of this world—and so do we.

Another time, Jesus healed a blind and mute man who was also possessed by a demon. This so unsettled the Pharisees, the religious leaders of the day, that they accused Jesus of calling on Beelzebub, the prince of demons. Jesus' response gives us insight into the opportunities that we, as Overcomers, have to take back what the enemy has stolen (see Matthew 12:25–29). The kingdom of God is *now*, and the strongman has been bound. This healing of the blind and mute man was a blow to the enemy and a trophy of triumph for Christ.

The thousand-year reign of Jesus is an image of the church age between Jesus' first coming and His ultimate return. In the meantime, the strongman is bound, and we are plundering the earth of his possessions with King Jesus. We have the power of Christ in us just like the seventy-two disciples—and we *can* witness victory over the enemy.

READ | Luke 4:14–21; Matthew 12:25–29; Luke 10:17–24

REFLECT

1. What was Jesus announcing when He went into the synagogue in His hometown of Nazareth and read from the scroll of Isaiah (see Luke 4:14–21)?

2. What was Jesus saying in Matthew 12:25–29 about the source of His power? What was He announcing to the Pharisees about the arrival of the kingdom of God?

3. How did Jesus respond when the seventy-two reported that even demons submitted to them in His name? What authority had He given them (see Luke 10:17–24)?

Could it be that Satan is currently attacking the world like a Mafia boss in prison? Could it be that he can't do much but make some phone calls? This means, Overcomers, the world is ours for plundering. . . . Have you ever thought of yourself as a trophy of God's grace? According to Colossians 1:13, you have been "rescued . . . from the dominion of darkness and brought . . . into the kingdom of the Son."[57]

4. How does knowing that Satan has already been defeated, and you have been brought into God's kingdom, liberate you to live as an Overcomer?

I know the word *plunder* might conjure up violent images, but this is violent stuff. It's important to not forget we plunder with the weapons of compassion, mercy, grace, healing, power, evangelism, and hospitality. Those are the weapons of our warfare, but it is violent, and it's been given to us to share in the victory with Christ.[58]

5. What are some ways that you can plunder the enemy and take back what he has tried to claim, destroy, and steal from you? When have you participated in freeing someone from the devil's snares?

PRAY | End your time in prayer. Ask God to remind you of the power that is available to you through Jesus Christ. Pray for opportunities to enter the "strong-man's house," plunder his possessions, and reclaim and redeem lives through the power of the Holy Spirit.

FULL ACCESS

There are so many things that we can look forward to experiencing in our new eternal home. The renewed heaven and earth. Our renewed bodies. Seeing our loved ones again. Meeting all the saints of the faith that have gone before us. Living an existence with no more disease, death, pain, or loss. But these will not be the *best* thing about the future glory that awaits us.

Our ultimate reward—the best thing that awaits us in eternity—is that we will have complete access to the presence of Jesus. As John related, "I did not see a temple in the city, because the Lord God Almighty and the Lamb are its temple" (Revelation 21:22). We will have unblocked and unfettered access to the very presence of the holy God.

Now, if you were a Jewish man or woman reading this in AD 96, you would have gasped at the idea. Throughout their history, there was only one place a person could go to commune with God. There was only one place on earth where it was possible to enter into His presence. That place was the temple on Mount Moriah in Jerusalem. It was where God chose to dwell. "I, the LORD your God, dwell in Zion, my holy hill. Jerusalem will be holy" (Joel 3:17).

But now, John was saying the *entire world* had become God's temple! In this new reality, we are positioned as physical bodies in a physical place in the holy of holies. We are ushered right into the middle of the heart of the triune God of the universe. Up to this point, our experience on the earthly side of things has been from the "outside" looking up. We have a little bit of the glory of God in us—about as much as our bodies can hold without exploding. But in this new reality, we will step right into the midst of God's love, holiness, and power.

We have been invited right into the very core of the Godhead. And not just us, but all of creation, so that we will live, dwell, and have our being in that place for eternity. Eternity isn't clouds and harps. It is reigning and ruling in resurrected bodies alongside our King and Savior in His inexhaustible well of joy and goodness for all eternity.

READ | Exodus 33:18-23; Isaiah 25:6-9; 1 John 5:3-5

REFLECT

1. How did God respond to Moses when he asked to see His glory? What did God say would happen if Moses were to see His face (see Exodus 33:18–23)?

> We are going to see God face-to-face. And on that day, what we will hear is "Well done.". . . There will be no condemnation for us, no eye roll, no loaded questions like, "What were you thinking?" No. We will see Him face-to-face. "Well done. Enter into your reward." In every way, by the grace of God, we should be living for this moment.[59]

2. What emotions swirl inside you as you imagine what it will be like to look in Jesus' eyes and hear Him say, "Well done, good and faithful servant!" (Matthew 25:23)?

3. What questions have you been saving up to ask God when you're finally face-to-face with Him? Do you imagine those questions will seem as important once you are in His presence?

> Seeing Jesus face-to-face orients the Christian life. Each moment is seen as a step toward this ultimate destiny. Each day, week, month, year, and decade is seen as a pilgrimage to this great end. This is the eternal bliss that awaits the Overcomers.[60]

4. What does Isaiah say about the day you will see God face-to-face (see Isaiah 25:6–9)? How should the reality of being in God's presence orient your life?

5. What does John say about you as an Overcomer (see 1 John 5:3–5)? As you consider what you have learned throughout this study, what does it mean for you to live as an Overcomer in Christ?

PRAY | End your time in prayer. Thank God for everything that you have learned and experienced in this study. Ask Him to help you use this knowledge and draw on this experience as you share the gospel message and advance His kingdom in the world.

CONNECT & DISCUSS

Take time today to connect with a group member and talk about some of the insights from this last session. Use any of the prompts below to help guide your discussion.

What is one thing that stood out this week about the eternal home awaiting you?

Which Bible verse or passage continues to linger in your heart?

What is one of the biggest takeaways you have from completing this study?

How do you view the book of Revelation differently now than you did prior to this study? What has surprised you the most about Revelation?

What changes will you make in your life because of completing this study?

WRAP IT UP

Use this time to go back and complete any of the study and reflection questions from previous days that you weren't able to finish. Make a note below of any questions you've had and reflect on any growth or personal insights you've gained.

LEADER'S GUIDE

The Overcomers is an eight-session Bible study built around video content and small-group interaction. As the group leader, your job is to take care of your guests by managing the details so that when your guests arrive, they can focus on one another and on the interaction around the topic for that session.

Your role as the group leader is not to answer all the questions or reteach the content—the video, book, and study guide will do most of that work. Your job is to guide the experience and cultivate your small group into a connected and engaged community. This will make it a place for members to process, question, and reflect—not necessarily to receive more instruction.

There are several elements in this leader's guide that will help you as you structure your study and reflection time, so follow along and take advantage of each one.

BEFORE YOU BEGIN

Before your first meeting, make sure the group members have a copy of this study guide. Alternately, you can hand out the study guides at your first meeting and give the members some time to look over the material and ask any preliminary questions. Also, make sure that the group members are aware that they have access to the streaming videos at any time by following the instructions provided with this guide. During your first meeting, ask the members to provide their names, phone numbers, and email addresses so that you can keep in touch with them.

Generally, the ideal size for a group is eight to ten people, which will ensure that everyone has enough time to participate in discussions. If you have more people, you might want to break up the main group into smaller subgroups. Encourage those who show up at the first meeting to commit to attending the duration of the study, as this will help the group members get to know one another, create stability for the group, and help you know how best to prepare to lead the participants through the material.

Each of the sessions in *The Overcomers* begins with an opening reflection in the Welcome section. The questions that follow in the Connect section serve as icebreakers to get the group members thinking about the session topic. In the rest of the study, it's generally not a good idea to have everyone answer every question—a free-flowing discussion is more desirable. But with the icebreaker question, you can go around the circle and ask each person to respond. Encourage shy people to share, but don't force them.

At your first meeting, let the group members know that each session also contains a personal study section that they can use to continue to engage with the content until the next meeting. While doing this section is optional, it will help participants cement the concepts presented during the group study time and help them better understand how humility will help them see God, themselves, and others more accurately.

Let them know that if they choose to do so, they can watch the video for the next session by accessing the streaming code provided with this study guide. Invite them to bring any questions and insights to your next meeting, especially if they had a breakthrough moment or didn't understand something.

PREPARATION FOR EACH SESSION

As the leader, there are a few things you should do to best prepare for each meeting:

- **Read through the session.** This will help you become more familiar with the content and know how to structure the discussion times.

- **Decide how the videos will be used.** Determine whether you want the members to watch the videos ahead of time (again, via the streaming access code provided with this study guide) or together as a group.

- **Decide which questions you want to discuss.** Based on the length of your group discussions, you may not be able to get through all the questions. So look over the discussion questions provided in each session and mark which ones you definitely want to cover.

- **Be familiar with the questions you want to discuss.** When the group meets, you'll be watching the clock, so make sure you are familiar with the questions you have selected.

- **Pray for your group.** Pray for your group members and ask God to lead them as they study His Word and listen to His Spirit.

Keep in mind as you lead the discussion time that in many cases there will be no one "right" answer to the questions. Answers will vary, especially when the group members are being asked to share their personal experiences.

STRUCTURING THE DISCUSSION TIME

You will need to determine with your group how long you want your meetings to last so that you can plan your time accordingly. Suggested times for each section have been provided in this study guide, and if you adhere to these times, your group will meet for ninety minutes. However, many groups like to meet for two hours. If this describes your particular group, follow the times listed in the right-hand column of the chart on the next page.

Section	90 Minutes	120 Minutes
CONNECT (discuss one or more of the opening questions for the session)	15 minutes	20 minutes
WATCH (watch the teaching material together and take notes)	20 minutes	20 minutes
DISCUSS (discuss the study questions you selected ahead of time)	35 minutes	50 minutes
RESPOND (write down key takeaways)	10 minutes	15 minutes
PRAY (pray together and dismiss)	10 minutes	15 minutes

As the group leader, it is up to you to keep track of the time and to keep things on schedule. You might want to set a timer for each segment so that both you and the group members know when the time is up. (There are some good phone apps for timers that play a gentle chime or other pleasant sound instead of a disruptive noise.)

Don't be concerned if group members are quiet or slow to share. People are often quiet when they are pulling together their ideas, and this might be a new experience for some of them. Just ask a question, and let it hang in the air until someone shares. You can then say, "Thank you. What about others? What came to you when you watched that portion of the teaching?"

GROUP DYNAMICS

Leading a group through *The Overcomers* will prove to be highly rewarding both to you and your group members. But you still may encounter challenges along the way! To help ease this strain on you and the group, consider the following ground rules:

- When someone raises a question or comment that is off the main topic, suggest you deal with it another time, or, if you feel led to go in that direction, let the group know that you will be spending some time discussing it.

- If someone asks a question that you don't know how to answer, admit it and move on. At your discretion, feel free to invite group members to comment on questions that call for personal experience.

- If you find that one or two people are dominating the discussion time, direct a few questions to others in the group. Outside the main group time, ask the more dominating members to help you draw out the quieter ones. Work to make them part of the solution instead of part of the problem.

- When a disagreement occurs, encourage the group members to process the matter in love. Encourage those on opposite sides to restate what they heard the other side say about the matter, and then invite each side to evaluate if that perception is accurate. Lead the group in examining other scriptures related to the topic and look for common ground.

When any of these issues arise, encourage your group members to follow these words from Scripture: "Love one another" (John 13:34); "If it is possible, as far as it depends on you, live at peace with everyone" (Romans 12:18); and, "Everyone should be quick to listen, slow to speak and slow to become angry" (James 1:19). This will make your group time more rewarding and beneficial for everyone who attends.

Thank you again for taking the time to lead your group. You are making a difference in your group members' lives and having an impact on their journey toward a better understanding of how they can truly be Overcomers in Chrst.

NOTES

1. Ida Tomshinsky, "The Art of Writing Handwriting Letters and Notes," *International Journal of Business, Humanities, and Technology,* 3, no. 8 (December 2013): 112, https://www.ijbhtnet.com/journals/Vol_3_ No_8_December_2013/12.pdf.

2. "Handwritten Letters As a Revolutionary Communication Tool," Boston University Center for Mobile Communication Studies, September 14, 2018, https://sites.bu.edu/cmcs/2018/09/14/handwritten-letters-as-a-revolutionary-communication-tool/#:~:text=One%20of%20the%20most%20basic.

3. Matt Chandler, *The Overcomers* (Nashville, TN: W Publishing, 2024), 24.

4. Chandler, *The Overcomers*, 26.

5. Chandler, *The Overcomers*, 27.

6. Chandler, *The Overcomers*, 31–32.

7. "Apocalypse," Dictionary.com, https://www.dictionary.com/browse/apocalypse.

8. Ibid.

9. Chandler, *The Overcomers*, 28.

10. Ibid.

11. Chandler, *The Overcomers*, 57.

12. Chandler, *The Overcomers*, 44.

13. Chandler, *The Overcomers*, 59.

14. Chandler, *The Overcomers*, 60.

15. Alan F. Johnson, *The Expositor's Bible Study Series: Revelation* (Grand Rapids, MI: Zondervan, 2006), 645.

16. Chandler, *The Overcomers*, 62.

17. Chandler, *The Overcomers*, 62–63.

18. Chandler, *The Overcomers*, 69–70.

19. Chandler, *The Overcomers*, 71.

20. Chandler, *The Overcomers*, 81.

21. Chandler, *The Overcomers*, 70.

22. Chandler, *The Overcomers*, 80.

23. Chandler, *The Overcomers*, 82.

24. "Schadenfreude," Merriam-Webster.com, https://www.merriam-webster.com/dictionary/schadenfreude.

25. Chandler, *The Overcomers*, 88.

26. Ibid.

27. Darrell Johnson, *Discipleship on the Edge: An Expository Journey Through the Book of Revelation* (Vancouver, BC: Regent College Publishing, 2004), 195.

28. David Campbell, *Mystery Explained: A Simple Guide to Revelation* (Dayton, OH: DC Christian Publishing, 2020), 75.

29. Chandler, *The Overcomers*, 91–92.

30. Chandler, *The Overcomers*, 93.

31. Alan F. Johnson, *The Expositor's Bible Study Series: Revelation*, 677.

32. Chandler, *The Overcomers*, 94–95.

33. Chandler, *The Overcomers*, 96.

34. Chandler, *The Overcomers*, 135–136.

35. Chandler, *The Overcomers*, 121.

36. Chandler, *The Overcomers*, 111.
37. Chandler, *The Overcomers*, 121.
38. Andrew David Naselli, "What Is Holiness?," *NIV Biblical Theology Bible*, https://www.thenivbible.com/blog/what-is-holiness/#:~:text=%E2%80%9CHoliness%E2%80%9D%20is%20commonly%20defined%20as,separateness%20that%20entails%20moral%20purity.
39. Chandler, *The Overcomers*, 140–141.
40. Chandler, *The Overcomers*, 139.
41. Chandler, *The Overcomers*, 155.
42. Chandler, *The Overcomers*, 153.
43. Dennis Bratcher, "Travelers and Strangers: Hospitality in the Biblical World," Christian Resource Institute, 2018, https://www.crivoice.org/travelers.html.
44. Chandler, *The Overcomers*, 145.
45. Chandler, *The Overcomers*, 143–144.
46. Chandler, *The Overcomers*, 158.
47. Chandler, *The Overcomers*, 157.
48. "Aphrodite," *Encyclopaedia Britannica*, https://www.britannica.com/topic/Aphrodite-Greek-mythology.
49. Chandler, *The Overcomers*, 184.
50. Ibid.
51. Chandler, *The Overcomers*, 185–186.
52. Chandler, *The Overcomers*, 188.
53. Chandler, The Overcomers, 8.
54. Chandler, *The Overcomers*, 180.
55. Chandler, *The Overcomers*, 195.
56. Chandler, *The Overcomers*, 192.
57. Chandler, *The Overcomers*, 206.
58. Ibid.
59. Chandler, *The Overcomers*, 222–223.
60. Chandler, *The Overcomers*, 223.

ABOUT THE AUTHOR

Matt Chandler is a husband, father, pastor, elder, and author whose greatest desire is to make much of Jesus. He has served over twenty years as the lead pastor at The Village Church in Flower Mound, Texas, which recently transitioned its five campuses into their own autonomous churches. He is also the executive chairman of the Acts 29 Network, a large church-planting community that trains and equips church planters across the globe. Matt lives in Texas with his beautiful wife, Lauren, and their three children, Audrey, Reid, and Norah.

ALSO AVAILABLE FROM
MATT CHANDLER

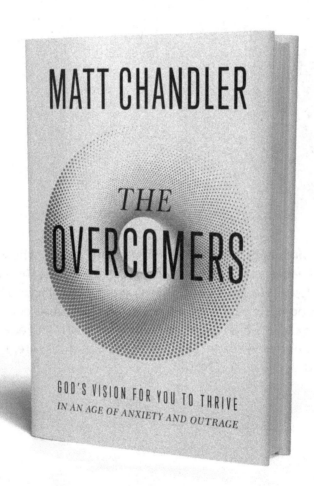

AVAILABLE WHEREVER BOOKS ARE SOLD.

W PUBLISHING GROUP